Abandoned to PhD

Integrating Meaning and
Resilience in Everyday Life

DR. GERALD C. BROWN

BALBOA.
PRESS
A DIVISION OF HAY HOUSE

Balboa Press books may be ordered through booksellers or by contacting:

Balboa Press
A Division of Hay House
1663 Liberty Drive
Bloomington, IN 47403
www.balboapress.com
1 (877) 407-4847

Print information available on the last page.

ISBN: 978-1-5043-8837-5 (sc)
ISBN: 978-1-5043-8839-9 (hc)
ISBN: 978-1-5043-8838-2 (e)

Library of Congress Control Number: 2017914519

Balboa Press rev. date: 10/03/2017

Integrating Meaning and Resilience in Everyday Life

This work is an autobiographical voyage through my life and includes wisdom and guidance to develop an individual's true inner compass - your thoughts, feelings, behaviors, self-awareness, motivation, and cultural exploration - while building resilience to find your life's purpose.

I write from my soul... If it was not me, if I was pretending to be someone else, then this could unbalance my world, but I know who I am.
Paulo Coelho

To venture causes anxiety but not to venture is to lose one's self...and to venture in the highest sense is precisely to become conscious of one's self.
Kierkegaard

This book is dedicated to my family especially my wife Barbara and daughters Lexie and Zoie who give me daily meaning and purpose to be the best man, husband and father I can be. My best friends Gilmore and Misti for their support, understanding, and unconditional acceptance of me. My past, present, and future patients whom I gather bits of wisdom from and who amaze me each day with their grit and resilience. All my mentors along the way and especially Dr. Wierzalis at UNC Charlotte for believing in me when there were darker moments I did not believe in myself. Last but not least Lambda Theta Phi Latin Fraternity Inc. for instilling important daily habits for success in my everyday life and really being proud to be Latino American despite the sociopolitical and cultural landscape we live in.

Contents

Chapter 1

Pura Vida!
(Not Accepting Circumstances You
Are Born Into: Birth to Adoption)

Pura Vida is not just a saying in Costa Rica it is a *way* of life…

Pura vida translated literally means "simple life" or "pure life," and these two words can be the underlying philosophy towards a more vibrant and marrow absorbing existence and life. One of my aims in writing this book is to include autobiographical elements throughout this book to permit a more genuine synergy between some of the concepts and ideas presented alongside my ongoing life narrative. Pura vida is also a way of paying homage to my *tierra natal* with an emphasis on never forgetting my roots in Costa Rica. In the spirit of never forgetting one's roots, one does not need to allow their roots to define the manner in which one lives and chooses to exist. Firstly, however I will begin with a brief description of my modest background in the little Switzerland of Central America.

I was born Danny Gerardo Morales de Trujillo in Caja Uruca Central in San Jose, Costa Rica in 1979. Costa Rica (Rich Coast) was so named by Columbus who *believed* the country was going to be a treasure trove of gold and precious metals (he later learned otherwise). San Jose, its capital, was named for Joseph of Nazareth and has many European influences dating back to the Spanish

Conquest when Columbus arrived in 1502. As one walks around San Jose, the distinctly European architectural influence is apparent. With a population of more than 200,000 people traversing its streets daily, San Jose is an important commercial and cultural hub. This relatively peaceful urban center is where my story begins.

The first few years after my birth I recall an insecure, and tumultuous childhood. Due to the short lived relationship of my birth parents, I was shuttled around from family member to family member including living with my birth mother, paternal aunts, my paternal grandmother, and lastly with my birth father and stepmother. (I use the term 'birth' to indicate biological parents as I was later adopted by my *true* parents). One specific memory is invoked from those trying first five years of my life and that is when I believe I was the age of 4, alone in my grandmother's house desperately trying to tie my shoes. I sat on the floor with tears flowing down my cheeks as I kept looping the laces in dozens of formations as frustration and anguish filled inside of me. After what felt like several hours I finally arrived at the solution and distinctly remember a feeling of pure accomplishment and relief rushing into my heart. This event of learning how to tie my own shoes is something I still hold sacred not due to the actual discovery, but more the fact that I did not give in to the frustration and desperation and kept working and working with single-minded determination for an end goal...

Many of us are born into less than ideal circumstances and yet we continue to allow those early experiences to abate our spirit rather than empowering ourselves. Remember that *now* you can change and *now* you can make more empowering choices to develop a more meaningful existence and cultivate abundant resilience for yourself.

Living with my birth father and his new wife was a challenging time in my early years as I felt very much ostracized by my madrastra (stepmom) and she would find ways to report to my father how badly I had misbehaved on most days upon his return from work. The fabric of my familial dowry became more torn as the resentment and frustration built up between my madrastra and me. Once my half-sister Luana was born I was completely replaced and was no longer important enough to my madrastra whom induced my birth father to desert his only son and commit one of the biggest cardinal sins of life. I was abandoned at age five by my birth father at a bus stop. I remember he had promised me an ice cream cone if I were to just wait at the bus stop for a few minutes until he returned. As the time passed I recall various individuals walking by including a mother and father walking along with their two daughters hand in hand, a group of nuns, and some older school children laughing and teasing each other. Time seemed to stand still until finally a bus came along and out stepped a portly police officer who directed me to *"ven conmigo"* or come with me. I began crying out of confusion and anger mainly because I felt cheated by my own birth father who had not returned with the promised *helado* (ice cream). I was sent to an orphanage in Heredia, a city with 120,000 inhabitants twenty minutes north of San Jose, to live until I was adopted two and a half years later. The pain of it now as I write this is more about the fact that my birth father did not have the boldness to explain or tell me his reasoning for the betrayal of his familial duty. For many years I wondered what had been so damaged about me but soon discovered even broken paintbrushes can still paint something beautiful and meaningful...

The orphanage I lived in was a one-floor ranch style home with four large bedrooms (2 sets of dilapidated bunk beds in each room) and one unemotional living room and kitchen including a large barren wooden table for dining and a set of rickety wooden chairs. I distinctly remember the stark, clinical white walls of the orphanage as if no youthful effervescence was permitted or existed. The chairs, concrete floor, and Spartan arrangement of furniture gave the impression of a home deserving of a loving owner. There was a small patio with one faded red bicycle and a few blades of grass fighting to exist in rocky and parched soil. The bicycle would be our one true luxury and we fought like rabid dogs to get some ride time. Sometimes those battles would become bloody and messy which would incite the ire of our strict Doña Malvolia to pull our ears away from the fracas and beat us all with her painful hand spankings. She believed that she needed to make an example of the bad apples by ensuring she spanked us in front of the rest of the kids to instill fear and control. One major discovery I later realized when potential adoptive parents were wooing me was that one of the other orphans in the *hogarcito* was my sister. Eventually I would get to know her; however it was not until age 7 that I fully recognized what having a sister meant and that she too had suffered abandonment. Ironically, the loneliness of the *hogarcito* pressed me towards a fellow orphan named Edmundo whom I grew to love as a brother.

Edmundo was a dark skinned boy with huge dimples and thick curls on the top of his head. His roots may be traced back to the Province of Limón on the east coast of Costa Rica where there is a large contingency of Afro-Caribbean peoples. Edmundo and I were inseparable as we subconsciously recognized the fragility of our existence and an instant bond of empathy and trust was established. My friendship with Edmundo helped me forget that I was *unwanted* because we both wanted each other. Edmundo was the first person who accepted me completely and I reciprocated the sentiment whole heartedly. One of my happiest memories was during a *fiesta* or party playing marshmallow on a string with Edmundo as we attempted to be the first one to eat the marshmallow in the middle of the string with our hands tied behind our backs. Edmundo and I would cover for each other as much as possible, especially when there were room inspections or if either one of us caused mischief or broke something in the *hogarcito*.

Edmundo and I would share the bike like brothers and we would play barefoot soccer in the back of the hogarcito until our feet and ankles turned a deep mahogany color (an earthy brown mixed with blood from cuts). Edmundo and I would play tag and escondidas (hide and seek) and when playing together the reality of our existence dissipated. On one occasion I remember breaking a coffee cup on the floor and Doña Malvolia slinked around the corner and demanded to know who had broken the ceramic cup. Before I could open my mouth, in jumped Edmundo and took the blame on my behalf. I still have not had a chance to make it up to him (I was adopted not long after that incident) and if I were to ever cross paths with Edmundo I would make certain to make it up to him. There are many silent moments in my life now when I say a prayer and affirmations for Edmundo and I hope he is doing well wherever and whatever life has demanded of him. We may have physically appeared worlds apart to outsiders but internally we knew the cruel pain of the undesirables of the world.

What I remember most about living in the orphanage along with ten other orphans were the potential parent visits. Time after time, parents from all over the world including the United States, Australia, and Europe visited our temporary domicile. They would walk in with their ornate purses and ironed suits as if visiting the zoo to peruse the grounds and the wildlife. As I look back now, it reminds me of times I have been to the pound and observed the melancholy behind the eyes of the puppies and older dogs. I remember a feeling of despondency mixed with excitement as privileged people would inspect us as we lined in single file along the entrance of the orphanage.

Those sort of memories *could* be drowned out by the cynical apathy of our Doña Malvolia or M as she preferred, who was strict and harsh with discipline. She was a woman with various premature wrinkles on her forehead and around her eyes, an acrimonious affect tied to past emotional and psychological scars from her own *vida* (life). She was particular about order and cleanliness and as a frequent bed wetter I made her livid on more than one occasion becoming more of a target for her cruelty and humiliation.

Once I recall trying to hide the urine by pouring water on the sheets to dilute the smell but she had the nose of a bloodhound and when she discovered my ruse she dragged me by the ear to the shower and put the shower on full blast with the coldest water one can imagine pouring down my hair and pajamas. I know that I received many *castigos* (punishments) by the Doña M but I choose not to recollect the darker experiences of the orphanage because I was able to internalize the physical pain into a longing for hope of a different life. My determination, friendship with Edmundo, and hopeful demeanor were pivotal in surviving the orphanage with only some degree of psychological, emotional, and physical scarring.

When I was an orphan, hope was the lifeblood of purpose and is all I really had. My story and experiences have informed my parenting skills and intuition as a father of two beautiful daughters. I use these memories as catalysts to empower myself and challenge myself to never abandon my daughters physically, financially, emotionally, psychologically, culturally, and spiritually. I *can choose* to be a bad father and have children whom I abuse, do not care about, or spend time with however; knowing the deep agony I went through with my own birth parents taught me to be a healthy and more resilient man and father.

The paradox of this tale is that many of the young men I work with in my current career struggle with finding meaning as men and fathers and thus choose life resignation over life resilience because they decide to *become* their birth fathers when the opportunity is right there to know how *not* to be a man and father. The following case illustrations demonstrate examples of life resignation and life resilience.

Case Excerpt of Life Resignation:

I once worked with a 30-year old Caucasian male named Chuck who had been sexually molested by a family member when he was 10 years old. This individual expressed that he had worked many of the issues surrounding this trauma out in previous therapy. As we talked more, I learned that the trauma was still holding him back and impacting how he chose to think, feel, and do. He constantly self-berated and sabotaged any positive growth or progress in our work or in his life. I finally had to have a major confrontational session in which I mirrored him in how he thought about himself, felt about himself, and the lack of any progress on our agreed upon goals and homework. This mirroring helped spur self-accountability within him, and he decided to stop blaming his past for his present thoughts and behavior. However, my instinct tells me that before too long he will be repeating the same cognitive narrative that he is accustomed to and regress back into anhedonia and life resignation. It appeared to me that he was the kind of individual that did not believe in himself enough to know that he could build on positive changes in his life so it was easier for him to digress in to external blaming and self-loathing.

Case Excerpt 1 of Life Resilience:

I worked with a 14 year old Latino male Domingo who was disrespectful towards his parents and teachers as well as maintaining Ds and Fs on his schoolwork. He told me in the first few sessions of our time together that he was not used to anyone listening to him. I saw some of myself in him and was able to use appropriate self-disclosure to challenge him to reflect on what he wanted and what he was doing about what he wanted. Borrowing from Glasser's approach, I assigned him homework on how he was meeting his needs for love and belonging, power, freedom, and fun. I stressed to him that he could only control *his* thoughts, feelings, and behaviors and not anyone else's. After three sessions Domingo began making new choices by deciding to do his homework, seek after school tutoring, and join student government as he wanted to give voice to many students' concerns. Domingo realized that he could always choose his attitude and that will propel him towards life resilience. I also challenged Domingo to reflect on how meaningful his life would be if he could consciously make choices that oppose the typical narrative of a young Latino male in this country. Domingo had never thought much about this but realized that he did not want to be voiceless and part of the emerging underclass of minority men with little education and opportunity.

As you read this book you will discover that you are composed of various elements (psychological, emotional, behavioral, perceptual, cultural, spiritual) of resilience or resignation and that *you* decide what you would like to include for your holistic self. One of the most critical facets of oneself is cognitive malleability because, as the 21st century rages on, one's thoughts have to follow the three A's of cognitive and psychological resilience: ameliorate, adapt, and anticipate. More will be discussed about psychological resilience and the importance of cognitive flexibility in the new millenium in the next chapter. Emotional and adaptive resilience are byproducts of a healthy and pliable thought process and includes fully experiencing one's feelings beyond the surface and being open to experiencing life with verve and purpose. Healthy thoughts and feelings lend themselves to action and risk for personal growth.

Meaningful doing and risk is derived from resilient thoughts and feelings of being open to experiences and channeling the rhythm of life. One approach to cultivating meaning and purpose in life that works with the various individuals and families in my practice is called the meaning journal. The basic premise is that each individual begins to reflect on how they make meaning out of each day and gains personal meaning through absorbing the spirit of life in all of its frontiers. Culturally, we all bring elements of our origins into this personal meaning and life journey. One theme I have found in my professional clinical experience is the avoidance of culture by mainly Caucasian clients but also by Latino, Asian, and African-American and mixed individuals. Part of the purpose of this book is to help individuals explore their cultural ancestry and roots. Knowing and understanding oneself culturally can be one of life's greatest pursuits and instructors. We will end each chapter with exercises on how we define our holistic selves via ongoing personal evaluation and finally how we can integrate all of our resiliencies as the 21st century thunders on with momentous transformation and foster influence on personal meaning and resilience.

Summary: This chapter covered pivotal aspects of my early life experiences that have shaped my ability to cling to hope despite darkness and despair. I illustrated two case studies to demonstrate how we as humans can make constructive or destructive life choices despite shadowy or unfortunate circumstances in their lives. Finally, I presented the topical outline of the rest of the book to help the reader understand the organization of this book.

Reflective Exercise:

Please make a list of 10 life affirming and constructive choices that you made in the past year (This may be a good exercise to complete around New Year's):

1._____

2._____

3._____

4._____

5._____

6._____

7._____

8._____

9._____

10._____

Now examine the list and identify one choice that you believe had the most impact on how you are living or moving towards life resilience. Write down the choice on a piece of paper and put it on your mirror, save it on your cellphone, or repeat it to yourself 30 times daily (or do all three).

Chapter 2

Psychological Resilience (Childhood and Adolescence)

I am responsible for the thoughts that I entertain in my precious mind
Bing Wilson

Shakira (my unacquainted sister) and I were initially being courted by a couple from Pennsylvania whom had sent us photos of themselves and their home. The photos revealed a welcoming brunette couple with similar facial and physical features as my sister and me. As I understand the story, the couple's relative was living in Panama at the time, and she agreed to visit the orphanage to be ears and eyes for the adoptive couple. Many years later I learned that the relative was not impressed with my sister's behavior, however, this was never explained to me or my sister why they stopped showing interest. At this point in my life I still had not been told that I had a sister and I think it may have been to *protect* me in case a family adopted my sister or myself but did not want the other sibling.

When I first met Shakira during that initial courting phase with the Pennsylvania couple, I thought that the couple just wanted a boy *and* a girl to adopt. Prior to meeting with my future parents I was more formally introduced to my sister Shakira. All I remember thinking was that I had spent all this time in this orphanage and *now* they tell me I have a sister…It went along with the disorganization and carelessness of Doña M and the foster care/adoption system at that time in Costa Rica. After two visits with these new *gringos* (Americans), my walls lowered, and I began embracing the idea of a new existence in my mind. My thoughts began to materialize and construct a hopeful reality of change.

Laura Peace and John Brooks came into our lives when I was 7 years old and Shakira was 5 in the summer of 1986. Initially, trust on my part had to be earned because these two individuals looked nothing like me and yet were willing to take me to *la casa blanca* (white house) in San Isidro de Heredia where they had been living for a year soaking up Tico culture and philosophy. Laura, my mother, was a tall blonde with hippie glasses and spunky attitude while John Brooks, my dad, was balding, grew a thick brown beard, and maintained a more reflective attitude. They later admitted that out of all of their expansive travels, Costa Rica was their favorite country.

The year-long courtship with John and Laura was eventful, stimulating, and filled with a lot of firsts for both Shakira and myself. They took us to places we had never been before including Playa Manuel Antonio, a beautiful beach nestled in the pacific coast of Costa Rica. They thrilled us with a visit to Parque de Diversiones (an amusement park) in San Jose, hiking along active volcanoes Irazu and Poas, as well as visits to more quiet destinations such as Guanacaste and Playa Palo Seco, unscathed by the influence of tourism. Shakira got a brand new doll whom she slept with religiously, and I remember the day I got my first toy, a Koala bear I named Binky, who stayed with me every night to keep unpleasant dreams away. When I slept at John and Laura's home I only had hopeful dreams. I vividly remember my dreams always including bright lights and feelings of warmth tingling throughout my body. These were dreams I wanted to cling to and re-experience in my daily living. Shakira was expressive and energetic although not coherent in her verbal communication. I had a difficult time talking with her because her vocabulary and fluency was profoundly delayed. As we begun to familiarize ourselves with each other we preferred smiles, winks, and other non verbals to convey our feelings as we came to realize we were going to have someone claim us and at least temporarily stop living in deep angst at the orphanage.

The flight from Costa Rica to the United States was incredible because I had never been on a plane before. Shakira and I sat next to each other feeling giddy about being on a plane because that was another incredible first for us. I recall looking down at my motherland in all of its savage beauty and the deepest blue of the Pacific sparkling back through my eyes as if to erase the hurt of the past and inspire new adventure. I observed Shakira sitting with a satisfied look on her face as the clouds meditated below us. Little did we know that when we arrived in our new home in Gaithersburg, Maryland I would not return to Costa Rica for 20 years while my sister has yet to return.

The first two years of my indoctrination into American culture were painful and frustrating for me. Two difficult hurdles were my name and the language barrier. I fiercely wanted to eradicate everything about Danny Gerardo Morales de Trujillo and fully embrace my new identity as Antonio "Tony" Brooks. My resilient thinking aligned with the idea that I can *become* Tony Brooks and recreate myself. My personal renaissance included my name because Mom and Dad asked me what I would like to name myself as I had vetoed Danny. The removal of Danny was appropriate in my life, and I felt empowered in those moments when I could *choose* my own name. My Mom and Dad seemed to be intentional in this exercise because they wanted to massage my self-reliant thinking and encourage the power of self-determination within me. American ethos is deeply planted in my psyche thanks in part to this decision. My parents literally pulled out a list of boy names, and I perused the list until I saw Tony and it immediately struck me as *me*. My parents agreed that Antonio is the formal version of Tony and so we agreed that Antonio would be my legal name and Tony my preferred name.

I remember the desperation I felt to belong but my broken English was a cause for automatic exclusion. Surprisingly, I do not remember being suicidal but am sure I experienced some suicidal musings during this phase of my life just because of the self-indignation I felt for my "Costa Ricanness". I recall wanting to talk without an accent and sat in the ESL class in Lakewood Elementary promising myself that I would forget all about Spanish and learn English better than native English speakers. Within two years, I was fluent in English and I had all but forgotten Spanish. During those vexing years I had no idea that I was eliminating a piece of the core of who I was. This was the beginning of my identity rejection phase of my life also known as the conformity stage, which in the United States according to Atkinson, Morten, and Sue (1998) teaches minority children who are not White, blue-eyed, and blonde to diminish their own ethnicity and embrace White culture. The identity rejection ultimately united with resilient thoughts, and Tony Brooks arose from the cultural fragments.

One of the most dynamic aspects of psychological resilience is self-esteem which refers to the value placed on an individual's own strengths, weaknesses, outlooks, skills, and principles (Morales, 2008). Some individuals appear to maintain an adequate reserve of self-esteem despite their personal and environmental limitations. Day by day, as I became more proficient with my English my self-esteem slowly stirred my self-reliance and confidence. One day I discovered another self-esteem booster and social game changer for myself. I was in the third grade sitting alone on the grass watching my classmates during recess play basketball. There was a foul on a specific play, and the ball trotted over to me. I picked the ball up and one of the boys asked me if I wanted to play. I shrugged my shoulders with a reluctant look on my face and stepped into the game. The ball suddenly found its way into my hands and despite never having played any basketball threw up a beautiful arcing shot that whistled through the net. From that moment on, I was the kid everyone wanted on his team. My self-belief increased dramatically that day and I will always have basketball to thank for that.

The beauty of sports is that with basic rules understood one does not need to communicate a spoken language rather a non-verbal intuitive language shared by many athletes across various sports and competitions (Yao Ming, Ichiro Suzuki and most international club soccer teams such as FC Barcelona and Bayern Munich).

In keeping with the sports theme, here is a case study about a young man who, through our work together, finally began to realize the power of choosing his own thoughts.

Case excerpt 1:

I once worked with a young African American male named Sam who was 15 and extremely talented as a football player. He constantly battled with his mother, sisters, teachers, and classmates because he would hold onto grudges and blame everyone else for slighting him and not taking account his role in the conflict. Through a cognitive approach I began poking holes in his false belief systems and helped him to see that he was living in the past a lot of the time and not focusing on the present or his future. I explained to him that he was experiencing Al Bundy Syndrome (reference to a TV character who constantly reminisced about his high school football days and did not do much to change his present circumstances) and that he could choose to become Al Bundy or rethink the present and future narratives for his life. We discussed how on the football field he was able to shed tackles and keep running while, in the game of life he was stagnant and getting tackled all the time by his grudges and hang ups. He slowly began to understand that on the football field he did not have time to think about the last play or last week only time to focus on now and the next yard to gain. I challenged him to begin applying that same mindset to his life, and Sam made a dramatic turnaround because he substituted yards for minutes and began living life one minute at a time through his choosing.

Short term memory and resilience

In my dissertation research I learned that individuals devoid of challenges and difficulty in the form of major life changes and commonplace events are not able to generate resilience (Brown, 2014) or not able to cultivate resilience meaningfully. Additionally, I discovered an unlikely element as a contributor to psychological resilience. All of the participants had learned how to have a *short term memory* for events, concepts, or activities that were negative or even traumatic (Brown, 2014). They experienced domestic violence, gang life, parental divorce, prejudice, cultural separation, poverty, and yet kept going because they did not allow the heaviness of their home life to consume their thoughts. In case excerpt 1 Shaun was able to develop that short-term memory resilience for himself and his thoughts became more present-oriented and empowering.

In my clinical and coaching practice I counsel clients to cultivate a short-term memory for the pain and anguish of life and store the pearls of wonder and pleasure in their long-term memory bank. The main difference between the two is in the duration of the memory and the capacity of memory that each reserve holds. Once the initial memory is received we sift through a complex process of encoding into three memory locations: short term memory, working memory, and long term memory (Cowan, 2008).

My argument is that individuals with more cognitive elasticity make decisions with memories before they pass on to even the short-term memory bank. I imagine almost like two doors leading to the hallway of memories one labeled enter and one labeled exit. Many successful individuals are able to redirect traumatic and adverse experiences, people, and events to the exit door where they leave and never return. This is almost instinctual and the instinct itself would have had to have been cultivated since childhood through positive thoughts and making the most out of each experience hostile or not. Some of these thoughts become memories but even still we all have *options* with memories in our short-term memory bank. I propose that more psychologically resilient individuals are able to sift through negative and traumatic events quickly and only store the images and memories for a short amount of time in short term memory before the memories are removed altogether or are placed in a deep recess of the mind where individuals *choose* not to reflect upon or visit. Author Philip Ball wrote an article on memory for the *Guardian* and how in the next few decades the possibility exists for people to edit their own memories or have false ones implanted. I am not advocating for artificial memory editing or replacement but I am arguing that many individuals are able to maintain an automatic trash receptor for negative or traumatic events.

This is not to say that the memories are ever completely erased (unless the thought does not even reach the initial corridor as referenced earlier) however, I am suggesting that it would take a lot of work for these individuals to go to that trash receptor and recall what had been discarded. There will always be some of the residue left over because autobiographical abuse memories like the ones described in the *hogarcito* in chapter one are hard to remove. During the process of writing chapter one I was suddenly piecing together the painful images (residue) of that experience.

Carl Jung (1964) posited that we have what is called the collective unconscious and that individuals can tap into their unconscious desires, instincts, thoughts, and feelings. He argued that individuals who begin to identify themes from their subconscious (dreams) and symbols and weave those themes naturally in their conscious world are able to create new meaning from past wrongs and sufferings. This subconscious and conscious equilibrium may be another way to understand psychological resilience.

Some authors argue that autobiographical memories of abuse,

neglect, abandonement, and other traumas are more difficult if not impossible to expel (Geraerts & McNally, 2008). They argue that a repressive coping style may do well in the short run by forgetting or repressing traumatic events or images; however in the long run the thoughts may come back in the form of intrusive thoughts that appear suddenly and without warning. Thus short-term memory may be one element of psychological resilience and the other is that the individual remembers his or her own value and self-worth after a trauma or crisis and this helps erode *or* repress the pain and the memory much faster. Individuals may experience psychological resilience to trauma or negative experiences in different parts of their lives and respond to the trauma based on how much they value themselves and whether they have integrated the darker parts of their subconscious with their conscious domain and have found new purpose and meaning from this assimilation.

In my experience with trauma survivors I have found that there are survivors who adapted and bounced back within weeks and while others were still visibly carrying the chains and scars of the trauma everywhere. There must be other forces at play that allow psychologically resilient individuals to keep waking up each day and embracing the challenges offered. Two elements of resilience on which I have conducted research are emotional and adaptive resilience, and I believe that psychological resilience paired with emotional and adaptive resilience are a triple threat of protective factors for us to utilize in our daily lives, as we will explore in the next chapter.

Summary: This chapter covered my early experiences of adoption and my early experience of rejecting my Costa Rican identity; which helped me cope psychologically with the onslaught of American affluence and privilege in which I found myself enveloped in abundantly. I included a discussion on integrating the subconscious and conscious in a meaningful manner, the benefits of short-term memory and importance of knowing self-worth as protective factors in promoting psychological resilience.

Reflective Exercise:

Please take a moment to reflect on what kind of bond and trust you have with your thoughts...

1. Write down some of the thoughts you have about the prompt above.

2. Do you encounter a good relationship and trustworthiness with your thoughts or is there room for growth in your psychological resilience?

3. One suggestion that may be helpful to practice is to repeat daily the following to yourself: I trust myself; I love myself; I believe in myself; I have the courage to face whatever comes my way today!

Chapter 3

Emotional and Adaptive Resilience (Teenager and Young Adult)

Feelings or emotions are the universal language and are to be honored.
They are the authentic expression of who you are at your deepest place
Judith Wright

I was a two-sport star during my adolescence, which helped me maintain self-esteem and cultivate emotional resilience during those tumultuous years. I remember playing select soccer and basketball and competing with some of the best athletes in the Capital region of Maryland. Every successful basket made and goal scored helped me feel validated that I did belong and I felt worth more and not less. I think the underlying theme of belonging substantiated my emotional resilience. Having been "chosen" to play soccer and basketball as opposed to "open" competition graciously allowed me to fill some of my emptiness from my abandonment. I am not suggesting that everyone needs to develop an athletic prowess in order to feel good about himself but each individual needs to find an equalizer or talent (e.g. acting, playing the piano, art, writing) that can buffer the potential pain and torment that comes with adolescence. During my late adolescence and pre-teen years I had worked so hard at being American and conforming to American values that Costa Rica had become a distant conception of who I was and where I had originated.

I started feeling uneasy about forgetting myself in middle school; thus another pivotal event occurred (during my 7th grade year at Robert Frost Middle) with the encouragement of my parents I began to take Spanish. I decided that relearning my mother tongue would be an excellent first stride towards remembering *me*. My 7th grade Spanish teacher Mr. Desperto awoke me to the beauty and energy of the language and the racial identity. This was the first time I remember seeing other kids and adults clamoring to speak Spanish and was taken aback because the past 6 years of my life I had been actively rejecting it and absorbing English. During my classes with Mr. Desperto my initial feelings of shame and embarrassment transformed to tingles of pride, which heartened my resolve to relearn what I had forced myself to forget.

Zolli and Healy (2012) alluded to resilience being the ability to build better boats in the volatile waters of the modern world with all of its complex processes and interconnectivity. My middle school and high school years were tempestuous at times but my self-esteem and self-worth guided me through the storms. During those years I was wholly unaware that I was adapting to the environment and not allowing the torrents of life to drown my vigor and enthusiasm for living. These two resiliencies were the cornerstones of adjusting to the challenges presented and helped nurture my adaptive resilience. The Spanish class and Mr. Desperto were the conduits or in this case my vessels to navigate the uncertain storms of my identity and renewing sense of self-awareness. If it were not for my feelings of emptiness and curiosity in the throes of middle school angst however, I may have never taken Spanish in the first place.

Prior to high school I moved to Raleigh, NC, which was a difficult transition for me as I had established roots in North Potomac, MD. I was not enthusiastic about moving to North Carolina as I was in a committed relationship with a Pakistani young lady who was also heartbroken when I told her the news. It took me about two months to recover from the break-up which I would say is the longest period of time I have been affected by a relationship break up. I believe it was the most difficult because she was my first true love. We had previously written to each other weekly letters and not long after the move to NC the love letters came to a halt. This was 1994 before texting, Skype, Snapchat, Twitter, email and Facebook were mainstream communication tools, so the agony was real for me; however I had to keep pushing on emotionally.

The first thoughts and assumptions I had about North Carolina were whether my voice and accent was going to change and I would be talking with a southern drawl within a year. I also feared I would only meet "rednecks" and they would not be accepting of me and my background. Prior to the move I was affected by toxic messages including the *fact* that all southerners are racist and homophobic from my Maryland friends and their families. I also feared that I would not meet people of various cultures and faiths of which I had befriended in Maryland.

Cary is a growing city situated just west of Raleigh, N.C. As I adapted to life in the south *my new home* began challenging all of the assumptions I had about the South and Southerners. At first I was hesitant to engage Southerners because I knew my accent would give me away that I was not from the South. However, I decided that I was going to be open to the experience of being in a new city, culture, food, and way of life. I will go into more details about these and other cultural experiences in chapter six.

Once again my athletic ability helped me integrate into a new environment which was foreign to my life experience to that point. I tried out for the soccer team at East Cary Middle on the last day of try-outs and gained immediate acceptance by making the team as the starting sweeper, or captain of the defense. I was able to grasp the momentum of that success to help me assimilate to the world of high school. I participated in other sports at Athens Drive high school including basketball and track and field, which softened the blow of being the new kid and helped boost my emotional and adaptive resiliencies.

Case Studies

I want to present two case studies of individuals with whom I have worked who have been able to persevere despite a lack of support systems around them. These two individuals developed healthy habits of mind, emotional strength, and intuition that continue to help them adapt to the 21st century demands.

William was a 14 year old African American male who came to me because he had been hearing voices, pulling his hair, and maintained obsessive compulsive behaviors such as avoiding public restrooms to the point that he would only use the bathroom in his home. This behavior ultimately led him to having serious digestive issues and gastronomic pains. On top of these issues was the fact that he was questioning his sexual orientation and sexual identity. His family was not supportive of his questioning status because they were all raised in the church to believe that anything but heterosexuality was a sin. He expressed to me that he felt alone without his family's support and the subsequent spurning from them affected him strongly. In those moments, I was the only friend and fellow human being who accepted him completely. I understood the great responsibility of my position and conveyed deep understanding, empathy, and genuineness. I helped him to increase his self-esteem through bibliotherapy such as Dr. Bret Raulson's *Coming Out Every Day*, encouraging Youtube videos, and positive affirmations. The core of his issue was his lack of self-worth because it had been trampled on by people who were *supposed* to support and not vilify him. After having a few months of work on his self-esteem his personal feelings about his sexuality improved drastically. William stopped hearing voices and reduced the amount of hair picking episodes dramatically from several times a day to two to three times per week.

After more time working together, the strategy of our work changed to helping William find resources like Time Out Youth which is an excellent organization in the Charlotte, N.C. region for young people looking for a place of acceptance. I encouraged William to surround himself with supportive people in his life as well as developing strategies for overcoming prejudice and discrimination even if that meant turning his back on his family once he became an adult. He is now talking regularly to his mentor at Time Out Youth and has met numerous individuals with whom to confide and share his story with.

William is an excellent example of an individual with adaptive resilience because he has battled numerous persecutors including his own family who have dismissed his truth as "a stage or phase" without fully accepting his insecurities or way of being. He has had to contend with the rejection of his way of being from his church and his culture. William needed other people in his life that would be in his corner. I envision William as one of the difference makers in the 21st century. As he develops into a mature adult he will continue his journey of becoming who he is and with the recent coming out experiences of public figures such as Michael Sam, Chastity Bono and Bruce Jenner he has told me that he is heartened to continue pushing onward.

I know how difficult high school will be for William but I feel that our work together on self-acceptance, finding meaning, purposeful living, and positive affirmations will help him to endure whatever odium obstructs his path. I presented him with the tools to ameliorate, adapt, and anticipate persecution and malignance to ensure his success in this endeavor.

Another population that is close to my heart are our nation's Veterans because many of the ones I have worked with are male, minority, come from disadvantaged backgrounds thus I can relate to them on a personal level. I have found that most of the Veterans I have counseled have developed a strong adaptive resilience. Many of these individuals have seen and witnessed unimaginable violence and gore and yet they still persist in their daily lives piecing their new identities together fragment by fragment. The following case study illustrates one such individual I met when I was working in a small college in Gastonia, NC.

Antonio was a middle aged African-American Army veteran who first came to my office with a fearful affect and a tense nature. He stated he had no family in the area and did not consider anywhere his "home." Despite having served his country for 8 long years he did not feel welcome in his motherland, and I felt his loneliness and was able to empathize through my own experiences of abandonment. He was going through 'culture shock' as some of his symptomology included anger over minor frustrations, feelings of helplessness, general distrust of others who were not Veterans, and learning a new identity after national service (Oberg, 1960). He entered my office with vigilance and conviction and sat down after rearranging his chair so that he could see me and the door. After three sessions Antonio opened up to me about his military experience and some of the obstructions he had experienced once he was discharged from the military. He spoke about encountering a new identity once he was out of eight years of service to his country. He had served in the Gulf war and had traveled the world but came back to civilian life broken with insecurities about how to re-assimilate. I approached his case from a humanistic-existential lens and helped him to begin reflecting on what his purpose and meaning was now that he was out. We spoke about death and suffering as a part of life and the shadow of human nature. Slowly, Antonio began to lower his emotional and psychological fortifications and trust the therapeutic relationship. As the semester and academic year progressed, Antonio's demeanor softened, and he revealed his vulnerabilities as an adult and asserted his strengths to continue growing into his incomplete identity. As he began to trust the process, he began trusting himself and examining his new identity through unfamiliar spiritual, cultural, emotional, psychological, and professional vistas. Ultimately, he completed his two year degree in Human Services and decided he was going to transfer to a university nearby to finish his bachelor's degree in sociology.

Both William and Antonio had learned to adapt as best they could to their circumstances and came to me for additional direction and to be validated for their life experiences. I felt like I was the person they needed in that period of their life in order to help them regain traction and purpose. The 21st century asks us to ameliorate, adapt, and anticipate; otherwise we are going to have a difficult time adjusting to frenetic society. Both of these individuals were able to answer the ongoing call of what life demanded and continues to ask of them.

My junior year of high school I began focusing more on my academics as I was only an average student and wanted to be competitive for college admissions. My long term adaptive thought process helped me foresee at that time that sports can be taken away at any moment through injury or other means whereas knowledge is power that keeps illuminating one's path despite suffocating darkness. I began trusting my ability to work hard and smart in my academics and with each A or B my emotional resilience was reinforced. It was around this time I recognized that I was not the smartest kid in the class but if I worked hard and did not give up I could make up for any intellectual deficiencies.

My high school years were turbulent, and I found myself connecting with my teachers more deeply than with my classmates. I attribute this to my status as the oldest son in the family and my earlier life experiences, which pushed me to mature prematurely.

One person that I consider my first mentor was my high school history teacher Mr. Bawm who was quite literally *the bomb*. He was genuine and knew how to speak at my level and made feel welcome in his classroom. He made his classroom his *home* where all who entered were treated as such. He helped me cultivate my adaptive and emotional resilience with his witticisms about life and taught me that a professional does not need to take themselves so seriously. I remember observing how he conducted himself in class and in the hallways where we would greet each other; he always seemed to be the same person no matter where I saw him. I hoped to emulate his approach of *being* in the world because I wanted to model congruence (his ability to balance his various roles) in my various identities and I was captivated by his basic philosophy of life. Now that I am a professional therapist I have read several books on Humanistic and Existential philosophy including works by Rollo May, Irvin Yalom, Victor Frankl, and Carl Rogers. All of these authors uphold authenticity and congruence in the therapeutic relationship. I owe part of my wisdom and success as a therapist to Mr. Bawm and my refinement to the aforementioned authors.

As I began inching closer to high school graduation in 1997 and 1998 I concluded that education was not something that could be ever be taken away and knowledge was critical in adapting to the upcoming century. As the 21st century moves forward there is growing evidence of more tolerant policies being put in place (the U.S. Supreme Court passes marriage equality as I write this book on 6/28/15); eradication of the Military's Don't Ask Don't Tell; Obamacare; Deferred Action for Early Childhood arrivals); however there are various impediments/organizations with ambiguous agendas that want to emphasize so called family values and socially inflexible policies and ideas. These groups want to limit women's reproductive rights and sexual minorities' rights to marry the person they love. The most insidious may be the suppression of voters' rights highlighted by the backward decision to amend the Voting Rights Act in June 2013, which allows jurisdictions (many with a history of questionable voting regulations) to implement voting processes and procedures that do *not* need federal approval from the Department of Justice. The rise of Donald Trump (now our President) has scared my own family, our Latino friends and neighbors, and the Latino clients I work with due to his discriminatory remarks made regarding Mexicans and immigrants in general. We fear that his beliefs and rhetoric are not in line with the 21st century cultural make up of our nation and in fact appear to create more division and alarm for Latinos, Muslims, disabled individuals, females and anyone who is outside the customary social U.S. norm (blonde, blue eyed, heterosexual, young, athletic, male, Christian, and self-sufficient). Now that he is President of our nation, the question to ask then is how can we as a society encourage our younger generations to build their unique resiliencies so they can keep up with the demands of the 21st century? Additionally, how can we as a collective people continue offering more progressive and inclusive policies to engage our increasingly diverse potpourri of citizens? The following are some suggestions as places to start so young people experience a richer and more diverse life from elementary years through college or technical training institutes. One important choice to make is making one's voice count through voting for congresspersons, senators, and presidents. Voting for individuals who are not scared of individuals from different backgrounds and life experiences and embrace the philosophy that change can be scary but the only way to grow. Additionally, middle and high school apprenticeships with a variety of employers and organizations, mandatory college visits at each scholastic level (elementary, middle, and high school), holidays that stress the importance of family (one week day each month for family), free higher education (at least through an Associate's Degree) and increasing funds allocated to workplace learning and mentorship programs in order for our young citizens to receive ongoing life guidance no matter their familial situations. It is critical to remember the following words so beautifully written by Bryan Stevenson in his book Just Mercy:

"The true measure of our character is how we treat the poor, the disfavored, the accused, the incarcerated, and the condemned. We are all implicated when we allow other people to be mistreated. An absence of compassion can corrupt the decency of a community, state, a nation. Fear and anger can make us vindictive and abusive, unjust and unfair, until we all suffer from the absence of mercy and we condemn ourselves as we victimize others—we all need some measure of unmerited grace."(p.18)

This chapter illustrated the importance of emotional and adaptive resilience via my own early life experiences in my adolescence. Additionally, I included two case studies to demonstrate clients I have worked with that exhibited emotional and adaptive resilience so that towards the end of our work together they were more capable of listening and trusting their own intuition and feelings about moving forward in their lives. Mr. Bawm was a comforting soul and mentor for me as I navigated the choppy waters of high school. I concluded by asking the question of how we can as a society begin emphasizing the importance of emotional and adaptive resilience as necessary ingredients for success in the 21st century and beyond?

Reflective Exercise: **Sentence completions**

1. Complete the following sentences with several endings of your own choice. These are just a few sample feelings. Add your own to the list. Possible endings are: My mother would, my father would, my brother would, my sister would, my family would, my classmates would, my friend would, my teachers would.....

When I was feeling

hurt

relaxed

teased

humble

laughed at

ridiculed

proud

embarrassed

confident

ashamed

_____

2. Substitute the x with all the above feeling words to make more sentences.

I felt x when

Example: I felt hurt when my brother would call me names.

Chapter 4

Doing and Risk
(Undergrad/Graduate School)

The biggest risk is not taking any risk... In a world that is changing really quickly, the only strategy that is guaranteed to fail is not taking risks.
Mark Zuckerberg

I remember the two-hour drive from Cary to Wilmington, N.C. to embark on a new chapter in my life. The voyage to my new destination gave me the opportunity to reminisce on the first 18 years of my life. Emotional numbness set in from so many sensations of sadness, excitement, hope, inspiration, and joy as I approached the modest coastal town and Schwartz dorm number 303 at the University of North Carolina at Wilmington (UNCW). I do not remember the feeling of being a babe in my mother's arms however, I do recall a sensation of the proverbial umbilical cord being cut. Upon arriving on campus my parents and I were directed to a large auditorium for an official welcome from the dean of students. My anxiety intensified during the obligatory introduction by the dean of students with the following statement, "Look around you folks one of the people either to the left or right of you will not be here next semester"! In that moment I made a covenant with myself that I would not be one of those in and out students. After a nice walking tour of the campus with my parents, we arrived at the family van. My parents were matter of fact about the symbolic departure; as soon as the Uhaul was unpacked they did not prolong the farewell as Mom gave me a hug and kiss and my dad a firm handshake and stated, "Good luck." They got in their Blue Nissan Quest, and as the van driving away the taillights appeared to wink at me and say, "Be a man and live how we have shown you to live." This was the beginning of my first expedition into true manhood, which was clumsy and lackluster throughout my undergraduate years.

That night I took a party bus to Wrightsville Beach and participated in a luau complete with a cook out and late 90s music hits with artists such as Snoop Dogg, House of Pain, Domino, 98 Degrees and other rappers and hip hop artists. I did not know a soul and kept myself out of the festive fray scanning the environment and taking in the significance of the day. My introverted nature prevented me from partaking in the celebratory atmosphere. I believe in those moments I felt a soft burning sensation in pit of my stomach all the way to my head. This sensation was familiar to the feelings of abandonment ten years earlier. After the party we were driven back to our respective dorms where I met my first roommate, a student named Jake who came from a small town near Fayetteville, NC. Jake was unapologetically Christian and was a self-declared "promoter of God" and let his enthusiasm for the Word determine his actions.

Jake and I for whatever reason did not bond from the outset, and we had a stormy relationship due to his constant preaching of the Word to me though I communicated to him that I did not want to be preached to. On one occasion I went with a group of dorm mates to Shell Island, N.C. for a night of undergraduate debauchery and returned inebriated to the dorm. Upon entering the room, Jake confronted me with passages in the Bible and condemned me as a sinner for underage drinking and Marijuana smoking.

We commenced with verbal scuffling back and forth about sin and personal freedom. I am sure I said some hurtful things during this argument but do not recall much except telling him to go find another roommate who was more in line with his religious ideals. Finally, he told me he would pray for me, and we went to sleep. The next day, as if God had been listening to our previous night's conversation Jake was reassigned to a new dorm, and I was happy to have an entire dorm room to myself.

This arrangement only lasted for a couple of weeks as I was soon assigned a new roommate who was more flexible in his religious and spiritual practices. In fact, I do not think he was very religious at all as the topic of conversation only came up when I first met him. I simply asked him not to preach his beliefs *unto* me and respect my own spiritual belief system (which at that time of my life had not been developed or addressed in any consistent manner). Kevin looked at me at that moment and said, "No worries," and that was the end of any spiritual or religious discussions between us.

Kevin and I had similar personalities, and I considered him a ladies man as whenever we ventured out of our dorm we would not go far before an attractive young lady would greet him or he would be invited to a party or get together later on in the day. I envied him and respected him at the same time especially since the entire UNCW female soccer team enjoyed his company. Kevin was accommodating and empathetic. He knew I was more reserved and he never pushed me out of my comfort zone despite offering invitations to me on a few occasions to party with him. I always made an excuse as to why I could not make it, unless my controlling girlfriend Marcia was going to be in town, at which point he knew not to ask.

I met Marcia during the waning weeks of my senior year of high school and we had a feverish blaze of romance that summer before college, which continued through my freshman year of college. She was a senior in high school when I was a freshman in college, so we only saw each other biweekly due to the two hours of distance between us. At the end of my freshman year, I moved out of the dorms and moved in with Marcia in an apartment near the university. That was when she began transforming into someone I did not know. She slowly became more suspicious of my whereabouts as if she did not believe I was attending classes. To be fair, I had broken our trust with a co-worker at the Food Lion I worked in through my high school years and admitted to cheating on her twice up to that point but she took it hard. She grew increasingly incapable of dismissing my unfaithful past. At the end of my sophomore year I was feeling constrained and dissatisfied with the arrangement and told her I wanted out of the relationship. I grew weary of constantly having to tell her where I was and when I would be home. There were numerous instances when I told her I would be home at 5:20 and if I entered the apartment at 5:28, she would want to know what I did in those extra eight minutes.

I recall the first time Marcia was sitting outside one of my classes and took me by surprise because I thought something had happened. After being dismissed from my Intro to Social Work course I spent some time talking to a few female classmates. Without warning she appeared and stared menacingly at my class mates. Her gaze communicated irritability with my classmates to which they awkwardly said goodbye. I asked Marcia if something had transpired, but she said she was there to ensure I was not lying to her about my class schedule.

In that moment I felt a sharp pain in the pit of my stomach because I realized that she was *actually* there to mark her territory as well as spy on my behaviors. These behaviors became commonplace, and she would wait for me after my classes on random days and times. I figured she would have done this practice for a month or two and then stop however; she continued to monitor me throughout the rest of my academic journey at UNCW. I had hoped that after a few months she would regain some of the trust that had been broken but she was just not able to put the pieces back together.

Early in my sophomore year my sister Betsy and her then boyfriend moved to Wilmington to begin a new life and to be closer to the beautiful beaches that lined the Wilmington coastline. Betsy was searching for herself at this point in her life and moving to live near her older brother was an excellent way to begin the process. Betsy and her boyfriend had a tumultuous relationship and they broke up and got back together several times. After a few months of the incessant asperity, Betsy decided living with her boyfriend was not what she wanted anymore. She and I agreed that she could come and stay with Marcia and I until such time she could get on her feet.

At first Marcia did not take issue with this as she understood that Betsy was in a difficult place. Betsy began working at a local pet store cutting and washing people's pets and truly enjoyed the work. The three of us would eat dinner together and talk about work, school, and life in general. After a few months however, Betsy and I decided we wanted to do some activities together as brother and sister. One night we planned a dinner at a local restaurant and upon announcing this plan to Marcia her eyes communicated panic. Something had struck her deep insecurities, and she began conspiring a way to alienate Betsy and ultimately force her out.

Betsy had been inviting friends and co-workers to the apartment more and more steadily as she was fast making a social life for herself. As time passed on Marcia would describe some of the individuals to me as unsavory and aimless (Most of these individuals would be gone by the time I arrived home). Marcia then began planting seeds about possible drug use occurring. I refuted all her accusations against Betsy up to that point. Marcia was cunning in describing how drugs in my apartment could derail my college and career aspirations. She began weaving that narrative, and I began to subconsciously question whether she was indeed correct about my sister's social connections and drug habits.

Marcia continued to instigate fear and finally decided to plant marijuana in Betsy's room under her bed. On that day when I arrived home, Marcia was inconsolable. I asked her what the matter was, and she pointed to the upstairs bedroom and escorted me to the small bag of marijuana peeking out of Betsy's mattress. In that moment I was consumed by anger and feelings of betrayal from Betsy.

When Betsy arrived home from work that day I told her to get out of my house and that she and her drugs were not welcome in my apartment. Betsy was dumbfounded and tried to explain that she did not know where the drugs had come from or how they got in her room. She pleaded and begged for forgiveness. I did not listen and allowed fury to make my decisions for me. Little did I know that Marcia had not only broken Betsy and I up in that moment but the ramifications of that day would seep into an estranged relationship with my sister for 5 years.

Kicking out my sister should have been a red flag in my emotional, cultural, psychological, and spiritual awareness. However, Marcia and I continued living together despite the warning signals flaring off around me. Another instance of Marcia's conniving nature and determination to maintain our relationship isolated was when I met a new neighbor named Mary. Due to our apartment's proximity to the university, the location was popular with many of the college students at UNCW and Cape Fear Community College. (As such I recall when a young brunette named Mary moved in next door a few months after we were living there. She was from Texas, polite, and very friendly.)

On many occasions, I would leave my apartment just as she was leaving so we would exchange pleasantries on our way to start our days. In one particular instance I arrived home after a stressful day at school and ran into Mary outside taking in the Wilmington sunshine and sipping some sweet tea in her sandals and sunglasses. As I approached the door she asked me whether I was a college student and I told her that I was pursuing Spanish and social work at UNCW. She and I continued to discuss UNCW and studies, Wrightsville Beach, and Texas barbecue. In the back of my mind I felt an anxious burst telling me to get inside before Marcia came home but alternately I was enjoying the discussion with Mary. Before I realized how long I had been conversing, Marcia slinked behind us and demanded that I check her tire pressure because she felt that the tires on her Volvo were a little flat.

When I returned from checking Marcia's tire pressure I entered the house and was accosted and lambasted about talking to Mary. According to Marcia, she had observed how Mary had been looking at me ever since she had moved in next door. I felt like a child who had just been scolded by his mother. Peculiarly, from that day forward when I saw Mary she would turn around and walk the other direction or ignore my greetings altogether.

Slowly I began to feel like I was suffocating just by seeing Marcia's face. I realized that she would have been happier if we had been living in some remote cabin near the Pisgah forest. This way no one would be around for miles and there would be no opportunity for me to stray and for her to maintain her coercion on my spirit. I began to try and make sense of her blanket insecurity and convince myself that she would soon begin to trust herself, me, and our relationship. I believe her father had been unfaithful to her mother as well and she learned some healthy and unhealthy coping mechanisms from her mother's advice. Her father was always at work and I believe Marcia observed how miserable her mother was by herself all the time and internalized that to mean that she needed to always be with me or know where I was.

Ironically, she became more and more controlling and possessive despite my efforts to appease her feelings of insecurity and jealousy. I slowly became more depressed and began questioning her motives as well. When she took a job as a cocktail waitress to help with the bills, we would argue about why she would be home so late at night. I started feeling resentful because I did not check up on her but she was allowed to continuously monitor and question where I was or why I arrived 7 minutes late to our apartment from class or the grocery store. We clearly were not functioning in a well-balanced relationship.

Marcia was the kind of person who always wanted the last word and never succumbed in an argument. She was convincing and knew what to say and when to say in order for me to agree to continue living with her. After, I begrudgingly agreed to renew the lease for another year with her, things went from bad to worse. During this time I fell into a deep depression and my weight ballooned to 290 lbs being only 6ft tall. I felt trapped in the relationship and smothered by her distrust.

In unhealthy relationships, one partner may maintain control by minimizing social interactions and connectivity. One of the things that Marcia was also adept in was keeping me from making social connections with others. There were so many opportunities presented to me including traveling abroad, joining a fraternity, participating in community service projects, joining the Spanish club, but Marcia's insecurities reigned strong. So I felt alone during these years, and my saving graces were my college courses, my therapist at UNCW, my dear friend Susan, and my parents.

Despite the darkness around me personally in my junior and senior years of college, I put forth a lot of energy into my social work studies and continuing my comprehension of my native tongue. I looked forward to my classes because those were the times I felt free of Marcia's possessiveness.

I particularly gravitated towards a professor named Dr. Rick who was a caring and unpretentious human being. He made me feel *valued* and not worthless, unlike Marcia. He saw something in me and convinced me to get involved in social work projects like project playground in which I organized and executed a community service project to repaint the neglected and dilapidated playground of a local boys and girls club. He also chose me to lead the hunger banquet sponsored by Oxfam America, which was a community wide event that helped the university and surrounding communities reflect on the maliciousness and pervasiveness of hunger in the USA and around the world. The academic and humanitarian experience at UNCW breathed purpose into my existence allowing me to tolerate the agony and melancholy of returning home to Marcia.

In my junior year I decided to participate in counseling at UNCW and met with a clinical social worker named Mr. Twain who actually greatly resembled Mark Twain with disheveled scraggly white hair and a long spiny moustache. He always wore a loose fitting suit complete with a yellow bowtie and tattered reading glasses. Mr. Twain was a gentle and soft-spoken man who validated my worth and listened to my weekly ordeals with Marcia.

Mr. Twain sparked my interest in becoming a therapist at the college level and affirmed my evolving goal to pursue a Master's degree in the future. Towards the end of our time together, in a quiet and solemn moment in session, Mr. Twain, who fashioned a non-directive style of therapy, abruptly broke the silence and exclaimed, "How painful it is for me to hear the desperation and anguish in your voice and I have arrived at the conclusion that the truest road in remedying your suffering is to get the *&%$^! out of the relationship." I then began taking steps to plan my escape from Marcia and most of the planning being psychological and emotional.

Another person who was integral in my growth and eventual separation from Marcia was my friend, Susan. I admired Susan, my 61 year old classmate, because she had returned from a nearly 40 year college hiatus. She was a native Wilmingtonian who had attended the University of Kentucky for a couple of years before getting married in her early 20s and raising six children while her husband drove a truck. Once she raised her six children she resolved to live for herself again and enrolled at UNCW to finish what she had started in Kansas. She conveyed determination, never too late to educate oneself attitude, and grew through risk taking. She was a true friend in the noblest sense of the word because she cared for me and challenged me to think about why I was remaining in a toxic relationship. My parents moved from Cary, N.C. to Melbourne, F.L. soon after my sophomore year of college so I was unconsciously looking for maternal and paternal figures that I could trust. Susan fulfilled my need for motherly direction.

Susan and I participated in our senior internship together as both of us were recognized as Child Welfare Scholars and awarded $10,000 each. During our internship we grew even closer, and I began spending more of my free time with Susan and her large family at her beautiful home ten minutes outside of downtown Wilmington.

Marcia did not mind because she did not feel threatened by Susan and her job as a cocktail waitress at a local night meant she could work late and bring home better tips. She would however call me when I was at Susan's to make sure I was there each night she worked late.

As graduation approached in May 2002 I approached Susan about leaving Marcia. I broke down and told her how things really were and that I felt trapped in the relationship. I remember how vulnerable and humble I felt during the conversation. I told her about all the suspicions, arguments, and her efforts to isolate me from the world. Susan embraced me and comforted me with maternal advice and tenderness. She stated that she suspected something had always been a bit off about Marcia but did not want to intervene in my personal affairs. We both decided to plan for my path after perdition.

The lease on the apartment was up at the end of August of 2002 so we agreed to designate the 31st of July as the getaway day. On that day, everything was to follow as if the day were any other day. Marcia would go to work around 5pm and return sometime around 1 or 2am while I would go to Susan's house as usual. This would give me approximately eight hours to pack my car with everything I could fit into my 1995 Toyota Corolla, turn in my keys, and have dinner with Susan before embarking on my liberation to Melbourne, Florida where my parents would be awaiting my arrival. Susan accompanied me to my apartment that evening in case Marcia arrived early and the police had to be called. After packing only the essentials of my life I stood back and stared at my car and reflected on how an individual really does not need much to live. I had my clothes, my books, photos, and toiletries. What I had most gained was not a possession or anything tangible, I had won freedom and permission to be myself, which comforted my soul in those moments.

Susan and I went to dinner together at Perkins Restaurant and Bakery on S. College Road, and I savored each bite of my veggie omelette, toast, and hash browns. I began tasting life again which slowly awakened me to the inner and outer vibrations of my existence. Our final stop before heading south to Florida was near a pier on the velvety sand of Wrightsville Beach. Susan snapped a few photos of me as I stood there with the ocean whistling and swashing behind me as the sun filled me with warmth and brilliance. From that day forward I began living with more conscious purpose, craving the more concentrated moments of living.

The drive to my parents' home was about 10 hours with an overnight stop in Savannah, Georgia. Even as I slept that night, I remember feeling anxious and hyper vigilant as I feared somehow Marcia had followed me. I looked around as if Marcia was going to suddenly appear out of the darkness in that small motel room. I awoke that morning without Marcia by my side and felt strange but free, not having to engage her or explain my itinerary for that day to her.

When I arrived at my parents' home in Florida, my mother was there to comfort me as only a true mother could. Little did we know the Marcia chapter was not yet complete. Each day Marcia would call several times to persuade me to come back. I spoke to her a few times and each time she would sound teary and apologetic. Finally, my mother instructed me to tell her that if she kept calling the home or cell phone any more that we would report harassment to the police. The last time I spoke to her I told her to stop calling or I would report her to the police and suddenly her tenor and tone switched from contrite to spiteful. She roared, "no one leaves me and I am not done with you yet, just wait and see!" These phone calls only solidified my desire to never return.

The day after Marcia's ominous warning and about two weeks into my return home, my mother answered a phone call from the Wilmington Police Department. My mom handed me the phone with an apprehensive gaze and I began speaking with Detective Johnson from criminal investigations division.

He stated that Marcia had accused me of rape. He requested that I return to North Carolina to discuss the allegations. We agreed on a specific time for our appointment and hung up. I glanced at my mother again feeling ashamed and like a failure but tried to cover up my feelings with a solemn posture and face. She held me in her arms and intuitively knew what to say and do to encourage me to be proactive. Following the phone call an hour or so later, almost as if written into a movie script, Marcia called and pleaded with me, "I did not want to have to do this but you left me no choice. Please come home and I promise you that I will drop all charges against you."

My parents were extremely supportive of me during this time as only parents can be and loaned me 500 dollars for a criminal defense attorney. I found an attorney in Wilmington, N.C. who agreed to accompany me to the police station the following week in order to explain my side of the story.

As I drove back to Wilmington, I ruminated on all of the possible scenarios that could happen. I reflected about the desperation of Marcia's bold accusations and how that could land me in jail. However, I balanced that thought with the fact that jail would be better than living with her. Another thought was how in the world was she able to convince detectives that I had done anything to her. I knew Marcia was manipulative and knew what to say, when to say, and how to say so people would believe her; however I could not believe that police detectives had been deceived as well. I pondered dealing with Marcia once and for all and not hiding or running away as I had grown accustomed to doing in our relationship.

One inspiration that helped me persevere may have originated from a dream I had experienced in those tumultuous two weeks. In the dream I was deathly afraid of a large, ominous serpent in a hallway that was blocking my path. I remember feeling frightened in my dream and desperate to pass the serpent. However, there were no doors or windows for me to escape so I knew I had to inch closer to the serpent. As I drew closer to the serpent I noticed its size would get smaller and smaller. At the point of reaching the serpent it was no bigger than a paper clip and with my right foot I stomped it. I remember feeling a huge weight tumble down from my neck and shoulders as I experienced genuine relief in that nocturnal reverie.

Detective Johnson was a portly and solemn Black man who sat down with me and my lawyer, Johnny Vincitore. Detective Johnson began explaining his experience in dealing with Marcia. The first time he met her she was hysterical and crying as she recounted her tales of being abused and raped by me on several occasions. He asked her why was she presenting all of this information now after I had left her, and she replied that she had been too scared to report for fear of reprisal.

Detective Johnson told my lawyer and me that right away things did not add up for him. First of all, most batterers and rapists would not come into the police station voluntarily as I had. He continued that she did not seem to fit the profile of a battered woman and that she seemed extremely eager to see me again and to try to work things out despite the fact that I had supposedly raped her on several occasions. He added that he called Marcia on three different occasions to interview her and each time the dates of the events, times, and abuse or sexual details were different. He declared that he felt she was desperate to get me back and would go as far as fabricating false accusations in the hopes of my return, at which point she would drop all charges.

I explained to Detective Johnson that she had called me the same day he had called and told me she would indeed drop the charges if I were to return to Wilmington and live with her. Detective Johnson told me that all that is required for a warrant to be issued is an individual going to a police station, sheriff, and or magistrate and telling their story of abuse or rape whether true or not. Detective Johnson stated that he did not issue the warrant for my arrest; rather the sheriff's office of New Hangarner County was responsible. However, he added that he would be glad to testify on my behalf if the case went to trial.

My lawyer, Mr. Vincitore, advised me that the best thing to do was to turn myself in to the sheriff's office and receive a trial date so that we could fight the false allegations in court. After turning myself in and going through a humiliating check in procedure including a mugshot, fingerprints, and changing into a jumpsuit, I was made to stand before a judge and declare not guilty in order to receive my future court date.

I spent the night in New Hangarner County Jail and mainly stayed quiet as I was housed with about 15 other inmates with varying offenses and lengths of stay. I remember dinner was the highlight of the day for many of them who had been there for more than a couple of weeks. One individual with a huge scar below his left eye and clean-shaven head approached me about my dinner. He introduced himself as Rocco and wanted to know whether I was going to eat the mystery meat on my plate. I told him he could have my portion and he thanked me and I watched him inhale the meat as if he had not eaten in days. I later learned from my lawyer that the date was set for January 11, 2003 the legal showdown in which I would finally be able to declare my innocence and unshackle myself from Marcia's shadow.

My trial date arrived in a fury and I met Mr. Vincitore in the main lobby of the New Hangarner County Court House and he told me that he felt very confident about the outcome and that he had already seen and spoken with Detective Johnson who was ready to testify if necessary. As Judge Freeman entered the courtroom I peered over at Marcia and her lawyer and felt a vigorous injection of buoyancy flush through my bloodstream. Marcia was called to the stand and began recounting the various episodes of sexual assault from her perspective.

Next, Mr. Vincitore cross-examined her and asked her to recall specific dates and locations and as he continued with his line of questioning Marcia burst into tears and sobbed uncontrollably. I believe that in that moment Marcia's guilt and anger burst out in her realization that this was going to be the last page in our chapter. The judge allowed Marcia to return back to the desk with her attorney. Mr. Vincitore called Detective Johnson to the stand, and the detective explained that from his notes from several interviews, Marcia had appeared to fabricate many of the allegations as she was not able to maintain a complete picture with dates, times, and locations of the assaults. Next, my best friend Susan took the stand as a character witness, and that she was able to relay to the court that I was a hard working newly minted social worker who was passionate about helping the less fortunate and had never witnessed me in anger or physically aggressive.

Mr. Vincitore's riveting closing argument included how he believed Marcia's actions were a ploy to have me return to her and then she would have agreed to drop the charges. He explained that Marcia had already confused and attempted to manipulate the Wilmington Police Department and that she was not going to stop until someone believed her subterfuge and duplicitous accounts of rape. I was impressed with the passion in his voice and the manner in which he delineated the various contradictions that Marcia had reported to detectives, the sheriff's office, attorneys, and the court.

At this time both sides rested on the case, and the Judge excused himself to review what he had just heard and proclaim a final judgment. Mr. Vincitore described the Judge as an honorable man who was also a Pastor and respected African-American professional in the community. He told me to take deep breaths and that from his perspective the Judge would not need much time to come to a decision.

Judge Freeman only self-deliberated for five minutes in his private chambers. Those 5 minutes were probably the longest 5 minutes of my life. I began reflecting on how I had gotten there in the first place and how I would never allow another person to diminish my worth and dignity. The judge opened his chamber door and slowly walked to his plush leather chair overlooking the mahogany and garnet décor of the courtroom. He returned with a declaration of not guilty on all charges. That buoyancy I had felt an hour earlier became pure adrenaline as I high fived Mr. Vincitore and gave him a hug and a kiss on the cheek in a way that only a free man could understand. The newfound freedom boosted my psychological and emotional resilience into overdrive. I celebrated by eating a complete portion of Chicken Parmigiana at Giorgio's and driving to the same sandy location on Wrightsville Beach where I had begun my exodus. I basked in the late afternoon sun and picked up the velvety sand to feel each grain slide through my fingers. The rhythm and the spontaneity of the transparent waves inspired me to continue following my inner compass towards purpose and meaning.

I applied to thirty different jobs the following day. I treasured the satisfaction of not having anything to hide any longer when I applied to various jobs and felt no shame about interviewing any more. Due to my emotional and adaptive resilience at this point in my life, I was able to continue pushing ahead despite the emotional abuse I had tolerated for so long with Marcia. I was able to identify individuals in my life who helped me to strengthen my resilience and help me find my self-worth again despite the clouds of gloom around me. This is a critical component to developing emotional and adaptive resilience because connecting with resilience building individuals (e.g. Susan, family) filled my emotional demitasse enough for me to act and make a change.

Nikita was a 32-year old breast cancer survivor who survived sexual abuse at the hands of her stepfather when she was between the ages of 8-12. She came in fearing what was next for her since her cancer was in remission and she had supposedly moved on from her past traumas. She described the pressure of knowing that many cancer survivors ran marathons, started businesses, wrote books, and took advantage of various opportunities to be successful. She had internalized that there was something wrong with her because she had no desire for advocating and proselytizing her survivor status to the world. As we continued working on building trust and rapport I learned that she had cultivated a failure identity since the time of her first molestation. She was an expert in sabotaging her progress in life despite also having attended medical school, visited and lived in various countries, and maintaining high levels of personal insight. Slowly we explored her shadow (Carl Jung) and I helped her to acknowledge and validate that part of herself. We also conducted an ongoing trauma narrative to help her manage and reframe her beliefs, feelings, cultural nuances, and spiritual aspects surrounding her childhood traumas. After months of work Nikita began to tell herself that she deserved more in life, respected herself, and loved herself. As Nikita improved her self-image she began trusting herself more and eventually risked moving away from Charlotte, NC to St. Raul in the Virgin Islands to pursue a medical career. She had previously studied in a medical school in St. Lucia and felt connected to the island life and we both agreed that moving back to that environment was a risk worth taking.

Leaving Marcia was a risk that I knew in my gut was right for me. If I had decided to remain in that toxic relationship I strongly believe I would have developed severe depression and would have contemplated suicide. My new chapter of liberation began with some professional thuds. My professional experiences led me to diverse job environments including moving furniture in the blistering heat of Melbourne, F.L.; working briefly as an on call child abuse investigator and Spanish-English interpreter in Wilson, N.C.; and even a pizza delivery driver in Goldsboro, N.C. All of these positions helped me remain humble and thankful for any opportunity that would come my way. In this period I recognized that I had an aspirational itch to return to school because I believed that I did not stand out enough with only a Bachelor's degree. I read reports about the watering down of bachelor's degrees and during a tight labor market how I would rise to prominent positions if I had only accomplished what is increasingly becoming a minimal requirement even for file clerk positions (Rampell, C., February 9, 2013). As time passed I knew I had wanted to return to school and decided to apply to East Carolina University. I realized that more education would only enhance my marketability and recognized within myself that becoming a counselor was a natural professional transition. Many of my co-workers and friends enjoyed talking *to* me because I listened and they encouraged me to pursue my dreams of mental health counseling.

In the fall of 2005 I enrolled in the Master's of Counselor Education program at East Carolina University (ECU). From the minute I stepped foot on the campus, I felt welcome from both the faculty and staff. I remember the very first day of classes being a bit lost and a nice older gentleman asked me if he could help me find the building I was looking for, he then proceeded to walk with me to the College of Education. In that moment I knew I had made the right decision because I had also applied and been accepted to another state university but did not feel the culture at that particular institution was a good fit for my personality.

During my tenure at East Carolina I matured intellectually, socially, culturally, and spiritually. I also developed an exercise regimen that improved my physical health tremendously. One of my most memorable experiences would have to be working for the undergraduate admissions office where I specialized in recruiting Latino families and their sons and daughters. I was blessed with a supervisor named Roberto Long who offered me carte blanche to develop recruiting strategies specifically targeted at minority students including Latino families and their children. I immediately began researching high schools in the region including Virginia, North Carolina, South Carolina, and Georgia with high Latino student populations. I called these schools and arranged a travel schedule to coincide with the dates I would be in that particular state.

I developed a bilingual presentation about the benefits of post-secondary education as well as the inclusiveness of ECU's admissions. I spent three months of each semester traveling and speaking to mostly Latino families and answering their questions and concerns mostly financial and process oriented. I realized that many of the students I spoke with had parents with no college education and some had not finished high school in their respective countries. This awareness helped me to begin reflecting on how to bridge the information gap besides traveling around as a one-man college coach with a lectern.

The traveling and speaking inspired me, and after much planning and consideration, it culminated in an event called Latino Student and Family Day. Planning this event was truly self-actualizing as Latino students who had applied and/or been accepted to ECU would be invited to the ECU campus along with their *familias* to take part in a tour, speak to professors, listen to administration officials such as financial aid representatives, and be provided lunch free of charge. About ten families participated, and I personally answered or connected them with staff to resolve any questions or concerns they had about academics, student life, extracurricular activities, and financial aid options for documented and undocumented students.

My academic experience at ECU was rigorous and entertaining. I especially enjoyed Dr. "X" who was an extremely brilliant research professor who used non- verbal antics to educate and entertain which made research classes so amusing. I never thought research could be interesting or even fun until I enrolled in his classes. I particularly recall his use of chalk despite the fact that we were in the 21st century. He clung to his chalk like a security blanket, and he would utilize so much chalk on the blackboard that the chalk would smother his fingers, nails, and wrists. He then would be in the habit of touching his face on his forehead, cheeks, chin many times so that by the end of the lecture he would look like a cirque du soleil performer.

Dr. Wellcome was my biggest supporter and mentor during my tenure at ECU. She was incredibly humanistic and flexible in her teaching approach. She invited me to her home and office on several occasions to talk about life, relationships, and my future goals. She was impressed enough with me that she asked me to co-facilitate some of her classes with her. During these times a seed sprouted in my mind about pursuing doctoral level training. What I took most from her was her humility and respect for her colleagues, students, friends, and strangers. Her accomplishments could have led her to arrogance, but instead she fulfilled the Rogerian spirit (Carl Rogers was a famous Humanistic psychologist who personified genuineness, empathy, and unconditional positive regard for people) that she had preached to us in her lectures.

During the last semester of my Master's program I applied to three universities for doctoral training. Dr. Wellcome was instrumental in guiding me through the process but also produced an impeccable recommendation letter on my behalf. My application was accepted for three separate interviews. One school was in Florida while the other two were in North Carolina. I had begun the process of applying to a school in Michigan but decided not to complete the lengthy application as by that point I had already completed various demographic information, essays, gathered research work samples, and submitted GRE scores all of which were time consuming and exhausting.

ECU will always have a special place in my heart as it was there that I developed a concentrated sense of psychological, emotional, and academic resilience and self-assurance. I believed then and now that it was the right choice for my first foray into graduate education. I gained abundant momentum and felt as a snowball on the receiving end of a gentle nudge down a winding and foggy snow crested mountain with snowflakes accumulating as much as my inner confidence. The blind ambition to succeed and keep rolling despite the unknown helped propel me to my next chapter of my self-prescribed education.

I was accepted into two doctoral programs and rejected by my first choice. This was the first time I had ever experienced rejection from an educational entity. As I read the denial letter my rolling momentum slowed and stirred my insecurity. I decided to frame the letter and use it as a positive. I put the framed letter on top of my dresser so each morning when I began the day I could reflect on the letter and incentivize my choices and actions. As time passed I learned I was not the smartest applicant or most talented especially after participating in three different sets of doctoral interviews. Nevertheless, I had two of the most significant ingredients to success in any daunting experience and those are: determination and time management. Armed with these two resilience builders I resolved to make the most of my doctoral journey knowing deep down I would not give up and I would stay on top of my time instead of allowing time to pin me down.

The fall of 2008 was a momentous time for me as well as the country. I dove in earnest into my doctoral studies as the same time that there was a young politician named Barack Obama running for president and taking the country by storm. His message was of hope and change, and I adopted that mantra as well for my life as my first semester of doctoral studies winded down. My doctoral cohort reflected the message of hope and change as there was so much diversity included in our cohort. We were immersed into research, writing, and presenting, and our class represented different ideas and perspectives. I learned about Ukrainian culture from Malena, Jewish and Hungarian customs from Kailynn, Hawaiian and Japanese culture from Jason, and life wisdom from Lisa, Henry, and Robert who were all in their 40s and 50s. My favorite part of the semester would be our cohort gatherings in which we would blow off steam, bond, and partake of each other's culinary offerings.

Jason and I connected on numerous levels as we were both younger, sport fans, and bilingual. Jason spoke Japanese as his parents' cultural ties dictated and he had visited Japan various times to explore his background. Prior to beginning my doctoral studies I visited Costa Rica for 2 weeks the summer of 2008, and I spoke with my fellow students about how nourishing that process was for me as I had not been back to Costa Rica since age 8. I will discuss more about this trip and subsequent trips back to my birthplace in the next chapter on cultural resilience.

Jason and I were naïve about the grueling nature of doctoral study and in the beginning we believed that we had all the answers because soon we would be newly minted PhDs. I remember thinking in my first year of doctoral study that I had learned most of what I had needed to know about being a clinician yet needed a bit of tuning and refinement. Our clinical supervisors at Ashbrook High School who trusted our work and allowed us free reign to run groups and other projects validated our attitudes.

As the semesters and seasons passed, my approach to my doctoral work transformed me into a more receptive participant in my coursework, internships, and life. In the fall of 2009 and spring of 2010 I also joined a Latin fraternity, which added an exhausting workload of responsibilities in addition to my doctoral work. This transformation was critical in my own internal cultural revolution. I am a proud Brother of the nation's first Latino Fraternity! The rigors of the initiation process helped catapult my resiliencies and my conviction to not give up on my studies and my future dreams. 2011 was the year I developed a more holistic outlook towards my graduate studies and most of my initial armor of superciliousness eroded to modesty and gratefulness. I began to trust in the fact that I did *not* have all the answers and trust myself *more* because of this awareness. The most difficult trial during my doctoral work was not the dissertation but rather the comprehensive examination (comps for short). I made notecards and read as much about multicultural counseling, theories, clinical supervision, and research as I believed necessary. I began a morning regimen of exercise with notecard review for an hour. I followed this routine for 4 months prior to the examination date.

The exam administrators were faculty in our program who chose two random questions on each of these four foci. I spoke to fellow cohort members and cohort 7 members about comps to assess my own readiness for the examination. The process was demanding and unlike anything I had ever experienced academically. When the day of the exam arrived and I could feel butterflies and hornets were buzzing in my stomach and the stinging pangs of apprehension.

I was instructed that there was to be no talking and we were allowed only bathroom breaks. No cell phones or other digital devices were allowed in the testing room. I walked in and sat down for the first of four "questions" and was instructed to only use the thumb drive and laptop assigned to me. I remember opening the first question which happened to be research and staring dumbfounded at the small laptop screen. I recognized that I was at the point of no return and would have to improvise most of the answer as neither question appealed to me or covered much of what I had studied. I remember feeling little balls of sweat slowly collecting on the small of my neck and underarms. As the first day of the exam finished, I went home feeling unconvinced of my progress. The next day was faintly smoother because I was acquainted with the comps process. When I went home after finishing the second day, I recognized my need for alcohol and unfurled with friends at a local sports bar.

Waiting for the results was agonizing. The days leading up to receiving my results were filled with obsession as I checked my email constantly both on my phone and any computer at arm's length. Two weeks later the results came in. My apprehension moved me to a discreet location in the college of education building where I could respond to the results in private torment or elation. As I read each professor's comments on my questions the heaviness began to press on the inside of my chest as I disentangled all of the written comments into full awareness that I had only passed two of four questions. My mouth opened wide, my shoulders shuddered, and I sat there for ten minutes bathing in disappointment.

That evening I loafed in my pajamas and lamented the anguish I felt in my chest. During these difficult moments I felt negative voices of self-doubt telling me I should quit, I am not good enough, and that I was *exposed* as an imposter in the doctoral program. The depression led me to put on my Netflix and I consumed three full episodes of Columbo to mitigate the disillusionment. As I continued watching Columbo ask "just one more thing" for hours on end I realized how persistent Columbo was at catching the killer. The next morning I decided to study in earnest for the exam by creating new counseling research and theory cards to review and read for two hours each morning. For the next twelve months I studied those cards each morning while eating, working out, or getting ready for work or school.

When I passed my comprehensives in January 2013, I knew deep down that my doctor of philosophy degree was only months away. I utilized a great resource called the *dissertation calculator* from the University of Minnesota Twin Cities. This allowed me to develop a timeline on developing research questions, selecting dissertation committee, writing the first three chapters, how often to meet with my dissertation chair, complete my proposal defense, defend dissertation, and bringing closure to the entire process. My dissertation involved in depth interviewing of seven first generation college Latino males and learning about how they were able to overcome various obstacles to pursue their educational dreams and aspirations.

At the beginning I remember being excited and nervous. The interview process was enlightening and touching. I felt privileged to have been able to work with these resilient young men and to peer into some very personal and delicate parts of their lives. With respect to analyzing and interpreting the data from the interviews I attempted to appropriately interpret the participants' stories and believe I accurately communicated their actual lived experiences.

Reading the interview transcripts gave me hope for the future of our country because I felt so blessed having the opportunity to listen to these young Latino men proudly speak about their struggles and accomplishments. At times I teared up reflecting on the story behind each participant. I also teared up at the fact that I realized I was only scratching the surface as to their collective lived experiences (Brown, 2013).

The lesson I took away from this experience can be summed up by stating that resilience means there are no finish lines, silver bullets, or final destinations…it is always provisional, long-term, and many efforts to achieve it will fade as new psychological, social, and cultural forces are brought to bear on a person. Resilience must constantly be reinvigorated and recommitted to. Every struggle at resilience buys us not certainty, but another day, another opportunity because every day is day one (Zolli, & Healy, 2012).

The important findings of my research included four specific areas of resilience that were found in all of my sample of first generation college Latino males including psychological resilience (particularly not conforming to a stereotype of what a young Latino male should become and self-confidence), academic resilience (mainly creating an academic compass, and understanding the importance of school), adaptive resilience (chiefly being adaptable and open to change), and economic resilience (primarily finding alternative strategies to finance education, and breaking the cycle of poverty).

Altogether these strands of resilience combined to benefit all of the participants at certain points in their lives and they continually foster an inner compass. What is important to understand from these findings is that all participants knew *when* and *how* to access each element of resilience at a given time and many times had to utilize *multiple* layers of resilience at once (Brown, 2013). They had been able to integrate the ability to ameliorate, adapt, and anticipate in their daily lives through moment by moment choices to improve their future and outlook on life.

As I was completing the interviews and analyzing the powerful words in the final draft, I broke down in a flood of hope, humility, relief, and sorrow. I recognized in those moments that my formal educational journey was soon to be complete and I would embark upon a new chapter of my life. The bigger picture from my dissertation spurred the belief within me that individuals who are able to integrate the aforementioned strands of resilience into their daily lives at the right moments are irrepressible no matter their gender, faith, culture, age, ability, sexual orientation, national origin or background.

This belief is part of the motivation for writing this book. My goal with this book is to inspire my audience to begin reflecting on how to integrate meaning with resilience and cultivate their own inner compass. The following exercise is a tool that can be utilized for anyone interested in a self-examination of their own resiliencies and areas where there is opportunity for personal growth.

Exercise for Chapter 4

The Resiliency Test

Part 1

People bounce back from tragedy, trauma, risks, and stress by having certain conditions/factors in their lives. These factors are listed below. The more times you answer "yes" to the statements below, the greater the chances are that you can bounce back from your life's problems "with more fortitude and adaptability." And doing that is one of the surest ways to increase your self-image and self-esteem...

Answer "yes" or "no" to the following. Then celebrate your "yes" answers and decide how you can change your "no" answers to "yes."

1. Caring and Support

_____ I have several people in my life who give me unconditional love, who listen to me without judging, and who I know are "there for me."

_____ I am involved in a school-, work-, faith-related, or other group where I feel cared for and valued.

_____ I treat myself with kindness and compassion, and take time to nurture myself (including me time, eating right, and getting enough sleep and exercise).

2. High Expectations for Success

_____ I have several people in my life who let me know they believe in my ability to succeed.

_____ I get the message "You can succeed" at work or school.

_____ I believe in myself most of the time, and generally give myself positive messages about my ability to accomplish my goals— even when I encounter difficulties.

_____ I believe I am unique and have special talents that no one else has.

3. Opportunities for Meaningful Participation and Growth

_____ My voice (opinion) and choice (what I want) are heard and valued in my close personal relationships.

_____ My opinions and ideas are listened to and respected at my work or school.

_____ I provide service through volunteering to help others or for a cause in my
community, faith organization, or school.

_____ It is important for me to accomplish meaningful and purpose driven tasks each day.

4. Positive Bonds

_____ I am involved in one or more positive after-work or after-school hobbies or
activities.

_____ I participate in one or more groups (such as a club, faith community, or sports team) outside of work or school.

_____ I feel close to most people at my work or school.

_____ When things get rough I have one or two people I know I can turn to for help.

5. Clear and Consistent Boundaries

_____ Most of my relationships with friends and family members have clear, healthy boundaries (which include mutual respect, personal autonomy, and each person in the relationship both giving and receiving).

_____ I experience clear, consistent expectations and rules at my work or in my school.

_____ I set and maintain healthy boundaries for myself by standing up for myself, not letting others take advantage of me, and saying "no" when I need to.

_____ If in a relationship I experience clear, consistent expectations and rules with my partner.

6. Life Skills

_____ I have (and use) good listening, honest communication, and healthy conflict resolution skills.

_____ I have the training and skills and know how to address any opportunities for growth to do my job well, or I have all or most of the skills I need to do well in school.

_____ I know how to set a goal and take the steps to achieve it.

_____ I have and affirm a vision statement for my life each day.

Part 2

People also successfully overcome life difficulties by drawing upon internal qualities that research has shown are particularly helpful when encountering a crisis, major stressor, or trauma. This can be thought of as an inner compass that people can listen to and trust in order to move in a genuine and positive direction.

The following list can be thought of as a "personal resiliency-builder" menu. No one has everything on this list. When life becomes challenging you probably have three or four of these qualities that you use most naturally and most often. It is helpful to know which are your primary resiliency builders, how have you used them in the past, and how can you use them to overcome the present challenges in your life. You can also decide to add one or two of these to your resiliency-builder toolbox if you think they would be useful for you.

Personal Resiliency Builders

Individual Qualities that Facilitate Resiliency
Put a plus sign (+) by the top three or four resiliency builders you use most often. Ask yourself how you have used these in the past or currently use them. Think of how you can best apply these resiliency builders to current life problems, crises, or stressors.

☐ Relationships—I am sociable/able to be a friend/able to form positive relationships.

☐ Humor—I have a good sense of humor.

☐ Inner Compass—I base choices or decisions on internal evaluation (I have an internal locus of control).

☐ Perceptiveness—I have an insightful understanding of people and situations.

☐ Independence—I am able to distance myself from unhealthy people and situations. I have autonomy.

☐ Positive View of Personal Future—I am optimistic. I expect a positive future.

☐ Flexibility—I can adjust to change and can bend as necessary to positively cope with situations.

☐ Love of Learning—I have a capacity for and connection to learning.

☐ Intrinsic-Motivation—I have internal initiative and positive motivation from within.

☐ Competence—I am "good at something." I have personal competence.

☐ Self-Worth—I value myself and have feelings of self-worth and self-confidence.

☐ Spirituality —I have a personal faith or trust in something greater.

☐ Perseverance—I keep on despite difficulty. I don't give up.

☐ Creativity—I express myself through artistic endeavors.

You Can Best Help Yourself or Someone Else Be More Resilient by . . .

* Communicating the Resiliency Attitude: "What is right with you is more powerful than anything that is wrong with you."

* Focusing on the person's strengths more than problems and weaknesses, and asking "How can these strengths be used to overcome problems?" One way to do this is to help yourself or another identify and best utilize top personal resiliency builders listed above.

*   Providing for yourself, or another, the conditions listed in The Resiliency Quiz, Part 1.
*   Having patience- successfully bouncing back from a significant trauma or crisis takes time and if you are patient with yourself the world will reciprocate
*   Having a selective short term memory- this is one strategy that many resilient individuals seem to have because they are able to keep pushing on despite past traumas and painful experiences (e.g. arguments that occurred last week)
*   *Self-forgiveness- having the ability to forgive yourself and accept one's own shadow as a part of one's life journey and that ignoring or dismissing one's shadow is to ignore and dismiss a part of oneself.

Keep in mind that if you feel that you are not as resilient as you would like there is always room for growth. Please pay attention to any of the above prompts or sections that you feel you would need to work on first in order to begin slowly cultivating various resiliencies. Congratulations on taking the first step by taking this assessment, reflecting, and learning more about you. I encourage you to participate in professional counseling or life coaching and taking this test with you in order to ignite the process.

Adapted from the following source: http://www.edu.gov.mb.ca/ k12/cur/cardev/gr12_found/blms/1-3.pdf

Chapter 5

Meaning Journaling
(Marriage and baby)

*Challenging the meaning of life is the truest
expression of the state of being human*
Victor Frankl

During my doctoral study I met a wonderful woman named Natalina
from Argentina who had arrived in the states in 2001 prior to 9/11/01.
We connected on many levels as we had both emigrated from Latin
America, spoke Spanish, and were young professionals. We met
while I was completing one of my numerous clinical internships and
she was referring Spanish speaking clients and their families to me
while I maintained an active clinical caseload in a local community
center (Mamie Moore) in Davidson, N.C.

We dated for a year and decided to move in together in our
second year. Moving in was a delicate dance because I was adopting
Natalina's daughter, Alejandra, as my own. Natalina was cautious
with introducing me during the first year but I became acquainted
progressively with Alejandra and explained she was fortunate to
have two fathers who loved her. At first I refused the label *step*father
because I viewed myself as her father and nothing less.

Alejandra and I competed for attention from Natalina, which I understood as a natural experience for an only child from divorce. Alejandra and Natalina had grown accustomed to spending quality time together thus after the initial warm honeymoon period ended between Alejandra and me, she began viewing me as an impostor. She continued to remind me, "I was here first!" Part of the stress surrounding our relationship was due to her relationship with her father who was reluctantly a part of her life. Alejandra was all in with her father, Mike, but sometimes he did not reciprocate and this impacted her self-esteem negatively. His own parents were constantly reminding Mike to be a father.

I felt torn between my duties as father to Alejandra and Mike's duties as father to Alejandra. As time has passed Alejandra has been able to become closer to me as her second father while I enjoy taking her on father daughter outings, helping her with homework, and talking about life and school. I believe that at times she feels guilty because she perceives herself betraying Mike. This way of thinking is especially true around the holidays when she is pulled in both directions and has to sacrifice one family for another.

I recall one Christmas where we were going to drive to Florida to visit my mother and Alejandra decided to stay with her paternal grandparents and visit New England. Natalina was hurt and I had to soothe both parties because Alejandra had a right to choose and Natalina had the right to hurt. My relationship with Alejandra helps me appreciate each day what my parents did for me because adopting a child as your own is one of the greatest acts of love in humanity.

Natalina and I groomed Alejandra months prior to our wedding and explained to her that we were in love and were planning to marry. Prior to the wedding we asked Alejandra to be a part of the ceremony as flower girl and she assisted Natalina in many of the logistical details including helping her with the design of the invitations and decorations. I recognized how Natalina complemented me because Spanish was an essential measure of her being and she maintained pride in her Argentinian roots. She studied Spanish and English in Argentina which led her to many opportunities in the U.S.

interpreting and translating documents. She challenges me to be a better man and father and continues to *corregir* (correct) my Spanish when I misspeak. In October 2010, we married officially at the courthouse in Lincolnton, NC. Naturally beautiful Lake Norman in Jetton Park served as our background for a modest wedding the next month with friends and family.

We became pregnant in the fall of 2010 and our daughter, Zelina, was born in May 2011. There is nothing that surpassed the pure and concentrated love and adoration that I felt holding my first-born child. In those moments, I began to develop a new meaning for my life. I made an internal covenant with myself that I would exist to mold my daughters into valued, intelligent, purposeful, determined, and humble human beings. As I stared wistfully into Zelina's eyes I reflected on all I wanted to show, teach, and foster within her. I recognized that this was my opportunity to construct new meaning as a father based on my own childhood experiences and accumulated knowledge. I tell myself each day that I know what *not* to do as a father and paternal caretaker of two impressionable daughters. I do not take my role as Papá frivolously and endeavor to redefine how I nurture my daughters as the 21st century reels on. I know how important emotional and secure sustenance is for my daughters and my purpose now is ensuring they receive plenty of it. I do not proclaim to know everything about being a father however; I am taking each day as a gift and I trust my inner compass to guide me in wisdom, love, and patience with my daughters.

As Alejandra has matured she has become closer to her biological father, which is truly a great blessing. However, that has placed me in a more clear and solid role of step-father with uncertainty about how to navigate this evolving role. Now she is 14 years old and no longer calls me Papá but I understand that she is cultivating a tighter bond with her father. The best thing for me to do is to devote one on one time with her as she continues to mature and develop into a bright young woman. I believe being a stepparent is one of the most difficult roles to undertake and it challenges me on a daily basis. The following case study illustrates the difficulties a father experienced adapting to divorce and partial custody of his two sons.

Jack is a Caucasian 52 year old divorced father of two young boys. He had recently learned about his Asperger's Syndrome diagnosis and was unsure how to endure in a meaningful direction. He expressed difficulty with effective communication and inadequate emotional resilience. Based on Jack's diagnosis we worked together to develop concrete goals to address communication patterns and increasing self-awareness of feelings and others' emotions. Jack was stuck as he did not enjoy his work, had been divorced within the past year, was adapting to his Asperger's, and was only seeing his sons once every two weeks on weekends. Part of the work involved challenging Jack to take a risk and quit his job without a confirmed job offer elsewhere. Jack quit his job and a month later successfully interviewed for a management position. During that month of unemployment I coached Jack on how to make the most of each day hour by hour. We created a weekly schedule that balanced job search time, exercise, spending time with boys, and me time. I currently work with Jack on raising his demands for more time with his boys as he is an excellent father but does not have the courage to confront the mother on custodial issues. Jack is a product of a system that is seemingly inclined towards maternal rights above all else.

Jack has to learn how his abundance of paternal capital is demonstrative of his resilience and communicate this to his ex, the courts, and himself in order to maximize time spent with his boys. The triumvirate of ameliorating, adapting, and anticipating are the batteries of the booster packs that need to be recharged daily. In this way I am able to put myself in my wife's shoes, Alejandra's, or Zelina's and be the most conscientious husband and responsive father I can be. In order to continue doing this I must also remember to take me time for myself each day whether that is 10 minutes or an hour or 16 hours. A long time ago one of my favorite professors advised me with her words of wisdom to remember to replenish my well each day and do not allow it to run dry. Revitalizing the well may mean different things for everyone. Physical exercise, cooking, cleaning, walking outside, traveling, playing with one's children, playing video games, social networking, reading, meditation, and yoga are just some examples of important resilience booster recharge strategies.

One exercise that I utilize continuously is called a meaning journal. I begin by reflecting on what I thought, felt, and did to bring value to myself and others each day. This process allows me the space and time to replenish my resilience boosters. I believe resiliencies are like booster packs that we all carry, and the more resilient we are, the more prudent we are with selecting which one or combination of resiliencies we need in a given moment. Meaning journaling is an excellent way to process the day but to also reflect on the direction that my life is headed. I ask myself where am I going in my life each day and pause for contemplation of my daily purpose and overall purpose. Currently, my purpose is to provide for my family and foster a sense of security, purpose, and growth within myself, my immediate family, extended family including close friends, and my community.

Exercise: Meaning journal.

Purchase a journal from a local retail store if you want added security you may want to purchase one with a key. If you prefer you can keep a digital journal on your phone, Ipad, or Laptop. Next schedule a 15-30 minute block of time each day in your smartphone, calendar, to do list, etc. to fill with meaning journaling. Now find a quiet place where there are no distractions and begin writing. Use the following prompt to get you started: I will bring purpose, meaning, and worth to myself and others through my thoughts, feelings, and actions today by....You may choose to write down a sentence or a whole page in the journal during this time. The beauty of journaling is that the space allows you to organize your thoughts and feelings into a tangible portrait of themes and subthemes of your life. When you recognize themes in your life that are preventing you from being more resilient in some feature of your life then you can begin changing your attitude, thoughts, feelings, and behaviors about that area of your life to promote positive change.

Chapter 6

Cultural Self
(We all have culture; some just
do not know it...)

Understanding ourselves culturally broadens our
horizons and the horizons of those around us

Cultural resilience is a relatively new understood strand of resilience that I believe is a crucial ingredient in my own ability to ameliorate, adapt, and anticipate daily challenges. Caroline Clauss-Ehlers defined cultural resilience in a holistic sense by stating, "Culturally-focused resilience contends that adaptation to adversity is a dynamic rather than inert process that includes character traits, a person's cultural background, values, and supportive aspects of the sociocultural environment (2004)." To expand upon this definition I contend that familial history and adverse aspects of the sociocultural environment are key elements in developing cultural resilience. I now want to explore my different cultural experiences since birth to explain further how I developed and keep developing my own cultural resilience.

My first real awareness of difference was a day that is emblazoned in my memory when I was an orphan at the Santa Barbara orphanage in Heredia. One day around lunch time at my local *escuela* (school) kids lined up to receive their daily portions of gallo pinto or sopa de pollo. I remember my stomach grumbling and I did not have any money for lunch that day but I was starving. I walked around towards the play area of the school and noticed some half chewed gum on the dirty concrete floor. I stooped down to pick it up and glanced nervously around to see if anyone was looking. When I decided the coast was clear I stuck the gum in my mouth and savored the faded sweetness and chewiness not caring about the grainy elements of earthly grime. I closed my eyes and kept chewing to give my taste buds the chance to savor the flavor. Suddenly, a boy with more means than I approached me from a corner of the school where he had been observing my actions. "*Cochino*" (pig) he called out to me and began laughing hysterically and snorting like a pig!

I turned around to face him and observed his snobby sneer tempting me to battle. Although, we all wore the same uniform of a white shirt and black pants his uniform was freshly ironed and cleaned whereas mine was a bit disheveled and worn. Unexpectedly, a blistering rage spread from my head down to all corners of my body and I lunged at the boy and tackled him into the rocky dirt. The fury unleashed within me possessed my fists and within seconds I was wildly pummeling him on his head as an excess of hatred and built up resentment flowed down my cheeks.

Within minutes there was a cheering perimeter of school children and finally, a couple of teachers arrived at the scene and picked me up off the other boy. Tiny crimson pools were splattered on the dirt and his shirt and pants just as ragged as mine. After the rage waned I realized I was an easy target; an outsider, vulnerable, I was one of the unwanted, and I was underprivileged.

The realization that I was part of the social underclass invaded my thoughts that day. Even as I received a cruel beating with a belt at the hands of the Doña that afternoon under a burning red sun in the back patio area, I remember staring into the distance and not feeling a thing. The numbness dulled the physical and emotional pain that made me feel like an indelible strand of my youthful innocence had been torn apart that day. In the days and weeks after the *lucha libre,* I retained an instinct to keep on fighting for me and those I cared about. Ever since that event I have preserved an underdog mentality in my life. I have developed a deep well of cultural empathy for the abandoned, forgotten, ignored, devalued, abused, and oppressed.

After I learned that I had a biological sister and that she was living with me in the *hogarcito* I recognized that I needed to fight for her too. I distinctly recall holding her when we learned that the couple from Pennsylvania rejected us. I could tell she really wanted the Pennsylvania couple to be our parents because they looked like us. As a Tico (term for native Costa Ricans) and big brother I naturally wanted to protect her from emotional and physical harm. Consoling her from the humiliation became my mission and cultural mandate.

When my adoptive parents Laura and John strolled into our lives I tried to model for her how we should behave by smiling and agreeing to as many things as possible. We did not know these people and they did not look like us but I whispered in her ear that we needed to get out of the orphanage and this might be our best chance. I had subtle awareness that at a certain age I would be unadoptable and my time was quickly approaching. Part of this reasoning came from knowing that there were other kids who were 2 or 3 years older than I that appeared angry and hopeless even listless at times. Trust and affinity would have to come later as right now we needed a home.

The underdog fighting spirit propelled me to adapt with cultural resilience when I moved to the United States. I remember the first trickle of culture shock occurred in 1987 when I climbed aboard a plane for the first time with queasy excitement. John and Laura had arranged for a small charter plane to take us to the national airport where we would board a commercial jet headed for the United States. As I entered the charter island hopper I recall staring at the white leather seats, convenience cup holders (not knowing what they were), and all the luminated controls in the cockpit. The pilot shut the doors, and 10 minutes later, we sped down the runway of La Fortuna Arenal Airport.

As we took off the pilot asked if Shakira and I wanted to fly over the Arenal Volcano which was a few miles away. As I looked down at the beautiful naturescape surrounding Arenal Volcano I felt a tinge of giddiness and exhilaration in the bottom of my belly. I glanced over at Shakira and winked as we both smiled, ready for whatever *La Fortuna* (fortune) would bring us in the next phase of our lives.

The flight from San Jose Santamaria Airport to Dulles airport in the DC area was smooth and providential. I cannot recall what I was watching as the in flight movie played but I could not understand much of it anyway as my English was limited to "hello", "goodbye", "how are you", "what is your name" and a few other greetings. There were many firsts on that early summer day in June of 1987. I had the privilege of flying in a private and a commercial airplane, eating lunch on a plane, using the onboard washroom (mainly for curiosity's sake), and setting foot in another country. Stepping on foreign soil for the first time I recall the onslaught of first world privilege and opportunity shocking my senses and awareness.

On day one of my transnational touchdown I felt a need to self-depreciate and become as inconspicuous as possible. This was the beginning of my cultural self-rejection, which pushed me to hide myself. I was entering the conformity stage of the Minority Developmental Model as developed by Atkinson, Morten, and Sue (1998, 2003). This stage of cultural identity denotes a sense of shame in one's own culture during which the individual desperately clings to the majority or dominant culture. This self-loathing implies avoiding and rebuffing others of the same minority, and include maintaining a discriminatory attitude towards others of a different minority. One of the first tasks Shakira and I did upon arrival was to consider new names. John and Laura seemed to have a plan with respect to our acculturation process and new names would give us a sense of choice and empowerment in a foreign land. John and Laura had a list of names from which they had been reading and presented to us. Since I did not like Danny it was an easy choice for me to change. I was struck upon hearing Tony and I immediately nodded my approval. To this day I feel special because I chose my name and recognize that most people are not afforded that opportunity. John and Laura had already discussed the names with relatives and John' sister Nadia thought Betsy would be an excellent name and was a comforting, American name. Betsy was only 6 and did not fully comprehend the process but she embraced her new name as well.

My low self-esteem was further buoyed when we arrived at our home in North Potomac, Maryland. Betsy and I got out of the 1985 silver Pontiac which was a limousine in our eyes and ran to our new two story house on Soft Wind Drive. The house was ginormous from my perspective and had a big porch on the back overlooking a sizable back yard that was fenced in on two sides. I heard a loud barking at the door and immediately my flight response went into overdrive. I wanted to stay outside until I knew Betsy and I were safe, but Laura took my hand and Betsy's hand and slowly walked us to the front door and in her excellent Spanish declared, "Bienvenido a su nuevo hogar."(Welcome to your new home). Laura slowly opened the door and out pounced the biggest dog I had ever seen with a fawn colored coat, rabbit like tail, and large menacing tusks as she growled at Betsy and I. Tica was a Bouvier des Flanders and overly protective of John and Laura. I lived in fear for the first week as she sensed my fear and took advantage. Betsy was not cowardly, instead she jumped at any chance to play and go on walks with Tica. Laura decided that if I were to begin each morning by feeding Tica our relationship would gain traction and a week of doing this Tica and I began trusting each other.

Betsy and I each got our own room and mine was decorated with Transformers bed sheets and pillow. One of my favorite toys was a Transformer that converted into an innocent looking blue egg. I spent many hours in my room those first few weeks absorbing all the changes in my life. Part of me was so grateful and excited but another part of me felt like I did not belong. Laura and John had also placed a variety of books in both languages on a little bookcase in my room. In my spare time I used them as an escape from the sensory excess of the new home, clothes, toys, food, and opulent culture around me.

There was to be a patriotic costume parade on the 4th of July, and Laura and John dressed the two of us in red white and blue themed costumes. I was Pinocchio and Betsy was Minnie Mouse. I recall a strong feeling of vulnerability and lack of confidence as I observed kids and their parents all around me marching down the tree-lined streets. They looked like their parents and spoke like their parents (without an accent) and this awareness made my insecurities bristle.

Fall 1987 brought on more trials as I spoke broken English and struggled to assimilate into the overarching American culture. Mrs. Panuchi was my 2nd grade teacher and embraced me as her favorite student from the first moment she laid eyes on me. She was passionate, strict, intimidating, and maintained a deep wisdom of life and meaning. She was an Italian grandmother and took me in as if I were her grandson or *nipote* in Italian. One of her primary goals while I was in her class, was for me to feel accepted and welcomed by my fellow students. In class I felt embraced and challenged to excellence. Outside of her class I was a loner and despondent because those were the times I felt most exposed. I was not able to communicate effectively with my peers and classmates and developed a strong suspicion regarding what other kids were talking, giggling, or laughing about. My paranoia led me to believe that I was the butt of their jokes and worse yet I did not know what was being said. I did not belong.

My ESL coursework was transforming me into an American day by day. As my English improved I clung on to my sense of conformity and White identified Latino identity (Gallegos, & Ferdman, 2001). Similar to the conformity stage this facet of Latino identity represents a tinted lens towards rejection of my Latino self and acceptance of White self. During this phase of my adolescence my cultural understanding integrated the ideas of conformity and

White-identified identity in a process to reject and abandon my Costa Rican cultural self.

My English improved so much and I demonstrated such progress that I was awarded an ESL award in 1988 for English fluency and grammar. Laura, John, and Betsy attended along with Mrs. Panuchi and a few of my classmates. That was one of my first memories of validation from others and that feeling of self-worth propelled me to speak perfect English. Consequently, I continued erasing Spanish from my daily verbal exchange as I moved between the two restrictive cultural lenses.

A documentary about slavery in America in the 4th grade forced me to begin challenging my desire to be White-Identified and conformist. The images of men, women, and little children being torn apart from families, whipped, and killed incited a visceral reaction within me. I sustained an internal dialogue with myself that began questioning whether being White was always a good thing. My reaction to the film emboldened me to read about Abraham Lincoln, Martin Luther King, John Brown, Harriet Tubman, and the struggle for equality for all people. Reading about slavery and the civil rights movement spoke to my innate sense of empathy for the forgotten, oppressed, and abandoned.

This social equality enthusiasm was bolstered by my cultural surroundings in my neighborhood and immediate communities around me. One of the cultural gifts that I slowly began to recognize was my neighbors and the various cultures they represented. My friend Maruk's family was from Iran, across the street Enrique' family was Colombian, another friend on my street was Jewish, and my best friends Pablu and Julio were from India and St. Croix respectively. The Stone Mill community was a beautiful montage of cultural influences. I met other children from Japan, China, Korea, Zimbabwe, Turkey, Egypt, Mexico, Chile, Panama, and many other nations.

I would go to my friends' homes and pay attention to their customs and cultural practices. I grew close to my Indian friend

Pablu whom I visited many times and learned about his native India. I had to take my shoes off to enter his home and I would watch his mother cook an Indian feast each night I visited. She would make my favorite Indian dish Masala Dosa paired with red Chutney when I visited on weekends. I would play basketball with my friend, Julio, and we would go inside his home where I had to greet his father as was customary prior to doing anything else. Julio's mother is still one of the best cooks I know, and her red beans and rice are authentic and delightful. Julio's family was from St. Croix, and were the most welcoming to my sister and I. In fact, my sister's best friend was Ariane, Julio's baby sister. Betsy cherished any free time she had with Ariane and they became inseparable.

I had a friend named Rook who was Sikh and was not allowed to cut his hair according to his faith and so he wore a turban (he had a few turbans to choose from depending on his mood). Rook and I played soccer together along with many other boys from Stone Mill and as diverse as we were, soccer was there to unite us as teammates and human beings. These are a few examples of the cultural diversity I was surrounded by in North Potomac, Maryland. I believe these early experiences cultivated a cultural curiousity to learn more about people's backgrounds. The following case profile is an example of how being curious of others' differences may open doors to trust, rapport, and cultural resilience.

Najiib was a Somalian client of mine who came to see me regarding difficulties managing familial and cultural expectations with American values and customs. The moment I met him he was wearing a dark winter beanie with an accompanying navy windbreaker despite the fact that it was 75 degrees outside. He was guarded and uncertain about the process and himself. He had recently finished his degree in biology at a nearby university and contemplating graduate school. Due to his early upbringing in Somalia and subsequent move to rural southeastern NC at age 12 he struggled with cultural identity and self-esteem. We studied and discussed aspects of Kim's (1981) Asian Identity Development Model and this helped him to begin normalizing his emotional, psychological, and cultural confusion. I was able to weave in elements of my own life experience in order to connect more fully with Najiib and build deeper trust. Since he was my first Somalian client I stated at the outset of our work that I wanted to learn more about Somalia and the culture of his origin. I noticed that by being curious and listening to him speak about Somalia and his early life experiences he rediscovered pride and appreciation which eventually replaced shame and avoidance of culture within. I helped Najiib process how to integrate the best of his Somalian identity with the best of his American identity to feel whole again. After some time Najiib stopped wearing beanies and windbreakers and began to love himself again instead of hiding from the world.

Laura and John had traveled around the world in their 20s and 30s and had decided to put off raising children until their 40s. During their various travels, they had collected diverse trinkets and collectibles to decorate their home. Betsy and I would marvel at the assortment of artifacts, instruments, and paintings sprinkled throughout the walls, counters, and rooms. Each piece was a memory and spun with a narrative.

My parents were able to recall one of the most memorable experiences in the following excerpt: One of the countries most notable to my mother was India – because it's teeming with contrasts and disparities, with abject poverty yet a wealth of spirituality. It's a land of lush fields, holy temples, picturesque mountains and crowded cities. She and my father traveled there four times together, both as "around-the-world" back packers and later as tourists on vacation while working in Saudi Arabia. India was truly the most inspirational, the most thought-provoking, and the most exasperating country she visited.

Mom remembers building a grass hut one winter on a beach in

Goa under the tutelage of the local inhabitants. They not only taught her and my father how to thatch the palm roof over their heads and how to protect themselves from crawling insects by wetting the perimeter with kerosene, but they also modeled a peacefulness rarely experience by Westerners. The locals possessed very little, but generously shared what they had. Mom now reflects: "If only I could live each day with such generosity." On another trip, Mom and Dad decided to travel by train from Delhi in the north part of India to Varanasi, also known as Kashi and Banaras. It's situated on the banks of the sacred Ganga River where Indians pilgrimage to wash themselves of their sins. For many, this sojourn happens near the end of their lives. The train trip from Deli to Varanasi is a long journey taking 12-13 hours. My parents decided to travel second-class to be more comfortable. In an effort to avoid the crowds at the station ticket office, they planned to purchase their tickets in advance.

Traveling from the hotel to the train station itself was eventful, since their rickshaw driver first took them to the wrong station. Eventually, after navigating through a maze of roads, assorted vehicles, and humanity, they reached the correct station and purchased their tickets without a hitch. The next morning they arrived early. Not finding a second-class car, they inquired at the ticket office and were told this train only had third class. When they asked why they were sold second-class tickets the day before when second class didn't exist, they were told by the attendant without hesitation – but with a typical Indian figure-eight nod of the head – "Because you asked for them."

The third-class train car had an aisle down the middle with groups of two short benches facing each other on either side. My parents sat on a bench across from an old woman reclining on the bench across from them. It was clear to them she was traveling to Varanasi for her last dip in the sacred Ganga River before her death. Mom felt a deep connection with and compassion for the lady. With each of the numerous stops more adults, children, babies and animals entered the train, until all the benches and aisle were bursting while others were hanging off the sides and seated on the top. The old woman could no longer recline and was propped in the corner with a baby on her lap while two adults and a young girl shared her bench and a goat stood at her feet filling the space between the benches.

Mom felt helpless and saddened that the old woman could not travel with dignity and respect. She had tried to protect the woman's space at first but eventually released her control of the situation. The journey on the train became a journey within as well. Mom realized why she was meant to travel by third-class that day: to face cultural differences head on by releasing judgement and attachment to her own beliefs and righteousness. She also realized she had no right to think she knew what was best for this woman and had no right in interfere. It was a painful learning. Mom truly believes our teachers in life come in many forms and appear when we least expect them.

The last Indian experience mom shared happened in the northeast region of India, called Kashmir, known for its lush valleys and awe-inspiring views of the Himalayan Mountains. Existing for many centuries with a peaceful co-existence of Buddhism and Hinduism, in the 13th century Islam became the prominent religion. Upon landing in Srinagar, the capitol, Mom and Dad were greeted by their travel guide.

Both of my parents were happy to have what they thought would be "a respite" from the confining cultural norms of Saudi Arabia where they were presently living. They thought the Muslims of India would be "less traditional" than those in the Middle East. During the whole day of sightseeing, when Mom asked the guide a question, he replied to my father. The guide walked in front of her, never to her side, and avoided looking at her face. Mom expected these gender roles in Saudi Arabia but not while on vacation. She was really looking forward to some relief from the constraints of living in a Muslim country.

Mom became frustrated and angry and felt belittled, even though she understood the guide's behavior intellectually. She considered herself a "liberated woman" and resented the "dominating male" treatment. She reflected on how she reacted that day so differently to behavior she tolerated in Saudi Arabia. Luckily, the Muslim influence throughout rest of Kashmir was not as strong. She considers the two weeks she vacationed in Kashmir to be among the most serene and satisfying of her life.

Middle school in Maryland inspired and expanded possibilities for me. I was still in my conformity state and White-Identified however, in 7th grade I enrolled in Spanish I with Mr. Desperto which provoked my sense of self to question what I had been internalizing about my cultural identity. Mr. Desperto was a fiery and outspoken teacher. Deep down he embraced, Latino culture, literature, film, food, music, and the various dimensions of culture tied to Spanish language. Never had I met a person of power that celebrated my heritage such as him. My inner cultural compass in that moment began shifting and racing inside of me.

Cultural dissonance is the process of an individual experiencing a conflict between self-depreciating and appreciating (Atkinson, Morten, & Sue, 1998). My 7th grade year plunged me into an undefined/other Latino identity (Gallegos, & Ferdman 2001) that oscillated from cultural confusion and not White, to denying the concepts of culture, race, and embracing colorblindness. As my Spanish improved throughout that year I began recollecting bits and pieces of Costa Rica. I became curious about my homeland and asked mom to cook Gallo Pinto for dinner as much as possible. I loved to watch mom cook the Gallo Pinto and I remember thinking that deep down she must have had a Costa Rican soul or been Costa Rican in a previous life.

First, she would sautée the Vidalia onions and sprinkle some olive oil with them. She preferred Goya black beans and would ask me to open the can. While the beans sizzled with the onions and pepper she would slowly add the rice and begin mixing. I would be responsible for mixing the rice and beans and cooking the huevos fritos (fried eggs). The eggs would rest on top of the gallo pinto with a few dollops of sour cream and cilantro garnish. Gallo pinto is a dish served any time of the day so I loved the flexibility and humble nature of the dish. The aromatic cilantro was a pleasant reminder of my cultural birthplace. Mom learned how to make corn tortillas by hand in her many travels in Latin America and so I felt fortunate to try her homemade tortillas when she made the time to prepare them.

Middle school incited new feelings within me that I had not experienced before especially towards my female counterparts. The summer before seventh grade was the beginning of my romantic awakening with girls. In summer camp I remember a female camp member passed me a handwritten note with a short and sweet note asking me if I liked any of the girls at the camp. I began looking around at all the girls and noticed one particular girl with long brown hair and sweet smile. My first kiss was with a Jewish girl named Anna the summer before seventh grade. Our relationship lasted just short of one month, which was, incidentally, the duration of the entire camp.

In August of the same year, my parents' friends had welcomed a Greek family into their home for a couple of weeks. During their visit I was able to become acquainted with their daughter Athena and Athena and I were attracted to each other from the second we laid eyes on each other. She was a couple years older but in the short time she visited we developed a hurried relationship. She stayed in our home a few nights and when everyone was asleep we slipped out to the local clubhouse and pool to walk and talk. There was a lake nearby with a meandering trail with rest benches that permitted us plenty of space to hold hands, cuddle, and kiss passionately.

Because my parents indoctrinated me with zeal for diversity and respecting everyone no matter their background, beliefs, or appearance, my romantic connections were as diverse as my friendships. As I began seventh grade I became brave and started talking with girls because the summer had energized me with confidence and curiosity. I dated a girl named Balzatala from

Turkey; despite a short lived romance that ended with heartbreak our relationship had different meaning for me.

Balzatala was the first girl to break up with me or as my peers termed the experience, "dumped." The break up hurt not only because it was my first dumping but because she ceased all further communication. A week passed before I realized what had happened as she had stopped interacting with me. I learned a painful lesson but I was able to bounce back. I met Gue from Zimbabwe a couple of weeks later and dated for a while. This relationship lasted about a month but as her brother was much bigger than I and went to school with me, our courtship was uneventful.

Next, I met and dated a Spanish girl named Sofia. I remember our first and only real date was when she, accompanied by her traditional Spanish parents, picked me up to go to dinner at a local mall. The date was uncomfortable as I tried to be polite despite feeling awkward and conversed more with her parents than her. She got mad that I paid more attention to her parents than to her, and I was axed again. Towards the end of seventh grade I met a beautiful Pakistani girl named Lona and I began sitting with her at lunch (this was the first indicator of interest between males and females at Frost Middle).

Lona was my first serious relationship as our courtship lasted about 6 months and ended towards the end of my 8th grade year at Frost. During that time we became close and enjoyed talking to each other especially about cultural aspects of our respective households. She told me that our dating had to be confidential in her family because her father would not approve of her seeing someone outside Pakistani culture. We had to nurture our relationship during school hours as I could not visit her home or be with her outside of school due to her fear of being discovered. The best time for us to be together was during school lunch so we valued every minute of the 45 minute lunch each school day. I wrote her sweet poems and she would write me back with equally sappy writings almost every day.

Our relationship ended for difficult reasons because neither of us could take responsibility for it. My parents, and specifically my father, decided around this time to move our family to Raleigh, NC. At that time in 1994, Raleigh was ranked as the best city to raise a family according to Money magazine and my parents bought into the hype. The impending move arrived swiftly as our parents were sharing information about the possibility of moving 6 months before the actual move in March 1994. Saying goodbye to Lona over the phone a week prior to our move was an excruciating moment for me, and I do not recall much of what was said as all I felt was pain and loss in my heart.

Chapter 7

Cultural Self Part II

In order to be universal you have to be rooted in your own culture
Abbas Kiarostami

Moving to Cary, N.C. a western extension of Raleigh, N.C. was tumultuous for our family unit. I utilized my adaptive and psychological resilience to navigate the culture of the new South. My sister, on the other hand, had a challenging time with the move and resented our parents tremendously.

The culture of the new South was interesting to me because in that time I noticed there was much less cultural diversity at East Cary Middle than I had been blessed with at Frost. I noted right away that the majority of the cultural make up of our new home was African American, Caucasian, and a small percentage of mostly Mexican residents. We moved to an upper middle class neighborhood which comprised of mainly Caucasian families with an Indian family and an African-American family. This was the first big setback to my cultural resilience because I had been so entrenched in cultural diversity that I felt I had taken a step back in time. Betsy did not warm up to Cary for a long time, and there were many nights when she and my parents would fight over trivial matters as deep down her protest signified her exhaustion of being uprooted from her previous "homes."

East Cary Middle afforded me the opportunity to move on from the heartbreak of losing Lona. In my early teenage male brain, "moving on" meant replacing old memories of girlfriends to make room for new ones. In a matter of four months I dated three different Caucasian girls. One who stood out for me was a girl named Amelie. She and I became close through a mutual friend named Rex. We hung out a lot at Rex's house because his parents were permissive and allowed him a lot of freedom. Amelie and I would play basketball together and especially enjoyed lover's HORSE in which the loser would have to oblige a romantic wish of the winner.

After a month or so of talking on the phone and spending quality time together Amelie told me she wanted me to come to her house to meet her mother. This was culturally important to Amelie as I wanted to be respectful, as we had great energy and mutual attraction. That day I got off the bus with at her bus stop and accompanied her to her home which was only a mile or so from my house. Her mother had not yet arrived when we reached her house. We decided to play a fast game of lover's HORSE prior to her mother's arrival. Thirty minutes later her mom pulls up and introduces herself. She takes a protracted minute to take me in and examine my physical features. The first question that came out of her mouth was, "Where are you from?" in a sardonic tone.

I gently replied that I was born in Costa Rica and had also lived in the D.C. area prior to moving to the greater Raleigh area. In that moment her mother gazed at me as she tilted her head to the side and abruptly went into her home. A minute later Amelie was waved inside by her mother, and I stood outside with a puzzled face. Amelie returned to me after eight or ten minutes with a flat look on her face. I asked her what the trouble was, and she matter of factly replied, "My mom will not let me date Mexican guys." I told her I was not Mexican and she stated, "to *my* mom you are like a Mexican so I am sorry but you will have to go."

As I watched Amelie disappear into her home I asked myself in my mind, "What the hell just happened?" There was no subtlety to the rejection-it was bold and piercing. A rush of sickness and dysphoria blanketed my entire body as I walked the long way home. I chose a shortcut through Lochmere golf course and as I walked I made a promise to myself to not date anyone with racist ideals or beliefs no matter their background. The rejection also spurred me towards the cultural identity development stage of resistance and immersion (Atkinson, Morten, & Sue, 1998). I began experiencing a conflict between feelings of empathy for other minorities and their experiences and feelings of ethno-centrism.

My freshman year in high school began with me questioning who I was and what kind of person I was going to choose to be. I was reconciling my status as subgroup identified per Ferdman and Gallegos (2001) as my race was unclear but my nationality, ethnicity, and culture were much more prominent in my everyday awareness. The first few months were tolerable because missing my great friends Pablo, Julio, Maury, Rook, Merced, Enrique, Sam and especially Lona hit me harder as my freshman year progressed. Without the benefit of social media at that time I lost touch with most of them. I felt like I was starting over in my life but this time it was without much opportunity to replenish my cultural resilience. My 9th grade year presented another interesting cultural event as during the same time the O.J. Simpson trial was taking place.

It was coined the trial of the century by many legal experts and news pundits. I recall the apprehensive days and moments leading up to the final verdict. Similarly to 9/11, most everyone remembers where they were and what they were doing when the verdict was announced. My freshman English class was dissecting Shakespeare when our teacher suddenly exclaimed that the verdict was in. All of the televisions in the school were turned on almost simultaneously. All eyes glued on every screen in suspense to hear the outcome of a case that had captivated the country for almost a year. When the verdict of "not guilty" echoed through the halls of my high school there was an abrupt and vivid celebration of all of the African-American students and staff bellowing throughout the classrooms, library, cafeteria, gymnasium, and outside. It was as if a collective cathartic release momentarily healed the wounds of injustice administered towards African-Americans in our nation. The trial had taken on a greater theme of race and culture and became bigger than one famous athlete's guilt or innocence. On the other end of the reaction spectrum White students and staff were stunned. I remember noticing White people crying and staring into the abyss.

I believe this was a candid snapshot of the cultural inclinations at the core of America. Watching the cultural dysphoria unfold helped me embrace my cultural heritage even more fervently. The resistance to the majority culture led me to distrust my White peers and befriend mainly African-American students. I became close to a good friend named D. D and I would have deep conversations about life, race, sports, and females. I would go to his house after school frequently and we would watch movies, play catch with a football, eat dinner with his family, and visit with some of his neighbors to play basketball and discuss current events. D's family was solidly in the lower middle class economic bracket, but they made me feel that I belonged in their home despite their lack of comforts and amenities. His mother was a Certified Nursing Assistant at the local hospital while his father worked for the city as a waste management specialist. They both worked extremely hard and provided as best they could for him and his older siblings. The family was economically resilient and I was impressed with how they made the most of what they had.

D's father would bring home barely touched furniture pieces and home accents to make the home feel cozy. I remember observing his mother come home and after a long day of work still have the kindness and patience to cook a delicious soul food meal and spread her love to D and myself. His father was a solemn man but humble and steady which I think is what I enjoyed most about D's friendship because he learned a lot from his parents about kindness, humility, and reliability.

One aspect of D that I noticed was that he did not have the

funds many times to go to the mall, movies, fair, and other paid events. I felt a strong sense of empathy for his economic situation and one day when I was in my parents' room I noticed a money clip with a bunch of 20s. I looked around to ensure I was not going to be caught and decided to take one of the bills and stashed it in my pocket hurriedly. This initial act also gave me a kleptomaniacal rush so that soon I became discreet and adept at removing excess bills from my dad's money clip. I began taking money regularly from my mom's purse and dad's wallet at opportune times in order to help my friend. I did not feel guilty about this because I knew that my parents owned their own consulting business and were making good money as independent consultants for major auto companies. Dad was the primary consultant while mom handled a lot of the day to day logistics.

I reconciled the stealing of my parents' money with any remorse as a way of taking a little bit from the haves and giving it to the have nots. I confess now to my wrongdoings as there were also times when I took money for my own purposes so robbing my parents was not always for altruistic motives. Looking back now I obviously know it was not the right approach to obtaining some spending cash or offerings for less fortunate friends but I also know that my parents never once asked or suspected any missing money.

My neighborhood in Cary, N.C. was culturally homogeneous except for the two other families in the neighborhood with cultural differences. One family was of Indian descent and the other was African-American. One afternoon I was walking back home from visiting a friend at Waverly Place (a small strip mall nearby) and ran into James, a tall and lanky teenager whose family had just moved to the neighborhood just like mine. I became close with James because he also felt somewhat out of place in the mostly Caucasian suburbs of Cary, NC. We would challenge each other fiercely in basketball games including one-on-one competition, HORSE, and around the world.

James lived about a five-minute walk away from my house in my neighborhood. On one occasion I decided to pay him a visit and his sister Missy answered the door. She told me that he was not home but, that she would gladly take a message for him. From that day on I started visiting James's house more often and eventually ended up spending more time talking with Missy than James. I remember Missy and James inviting me for lunch or dinner on several occasions which would normally be a Caribbean tour of tastes whether red beans and rice, jerk chicken, stewed cabbage, or fried or stewed fish. It was all delicious and through the food I felt like I belonged there despite the monocultural aspects of Cary surrounding us. The sense of culture in Missy and James's home inspired memories of Maryland and became a refuge for me.

Though James and I would remain friends, Missy and I had a lot in common and we just clicked. Missy and I both played basketball in high school, which provided another common thread to unite us. We often played one on one with each other to push each other to be better. Cary, N.C. in the late 90s was still finding its own identity. There were still remnants of the old South colliding with the influx of Northerners and differing values. Missy and I enjoyed spending time together but the more time we spent together the more we each experienced some of the dark residue of the old South.

I recently spoke with Missy as we still keep in touch to this day, and she recalled a time that stands out in her memories when discrimination knocked both of us psychologically and emotionally. We were walking through Lochmere golf course in Cary, N.C. nearing dusk on a steamy day in the depths of July. As we approached the walking trail behind our homes a middle aged White man approached us and asked us, "What are *you* doing here at this time of night?" "You both don't *belong* here!" We explained to the man that we lived in the subdivision 5 minutes away. He looked at both of us incredulously and got on his walkie talkie to verify our story. Once he confirmed our last names and addresses, his demeanor changed from a racist, aphoristic tone to a southern genteel, "You can never be too careful and I hope y'all get home safe now."

I looked in Missy's eyes. I saw the anguish behind her eyes, and felt so helpless in the situation. I wanted to say something but we both walked home in solemn silence shuddering from the antipathy and while this experience and others with her were blatantly oppressive, our relationship only strengthened in resolve and cultural connectedness.

Another example of an experience I distinctly remember is when we spent a leisurely Saturday afternoon and evening at a local strip mall called Waverly Place. We walked into a submarine sandwich shop and as we entered I could feel stares piercing through us. The glares signified astonishment and disgust at the two of us walking in together. We ordered our subs and sat down together as the questioning looks continued. I could not help but reflect on the feeling of disconnect and prejudice that was still alive in the region.

These and other experiences with Missy spurred me to the third stage of resistance and immersion in which I began challenging many of the dominant narratives of society that I had been fed up to high school. I began reflecting on why my ESOL teacher in 2nd grade pushed me so hard to learn English and forget Spanish. I questioned my parents' motives behind allowing me to forget Spanish and not insisting on a bilingual/bicultural household. I started to feel a sense of shame about becoming so Americanized and not acknowledging my cultural roots enough.

In my inner cultural conflict, I chose only to be around minorities for the majority of my school time and outside of school. I sensed more connectivity with the underdogs and those of modest backgrounds. This inner turmoil continued through high school and despite my skepticism and at times rejection of Caucasian individuals I still felt like I did not fully belong with my African-American peers. I recognized that in my high school there were Latinos but the majority of them were in ESL courses and seemed more interested in goofing around, skipping classes, and smoking than appreciating the opportunity to learn English and advance.

High school was an interesting cultural experiment for me and upon graduating, I felt a spiritual sigh of relief that the culturally awkward time was over while I was preparing for the next chapter of my life: College. UNC Wilmington (UNCW) in 2014 had about a 7% Latino student enrollment rate. In 1998 when I was a freshman I probably could have counted on two hands how many Latinos were enrolled.

As a typical freshman my mind was focused on other amenities that UNCW had to offer including an attractive campus, nice weather, two hours away from Raleigh, and Wrightsville Beach was 10 minutes from campus. I did not reflect much about the social aspects of college as I also chose UNCW for its rigorous academic reputation. As I became well entrenched in the UNCW educational culture I was equally disconnected from its social and personal culture.

UNCW was culturally homogeneous at that time and as I mentioned in Chapter 4 my introversion took over so I became a hermit, mainly staying in my dorm watching TV and fearing to try new things during my freshman year. I declared as a Spanish major first but did not feel confident in my employability after graduation so I explored other majors. My thinking was that Spanish was a great asset to have but not as big of a selling point unless I had Spanish combined with other skills.

I took a class with Donna Bene in 2000 in my sophomore year called introduction to social work and my academic compass pointed towards the department of social work at UNCW. She was a no holds barred liberal and filled the room with passion for social justice. She inspired me to declare as a social work major and to be an advocate for the less fortunate in the Wilmington community.

I became embedded in the world of social work and was fascinated by the diverse experiences of my professors. One professor, Dr. B had been a homeless Veteran and then began his long journey into graduate school to advocate for socially disadvantaged families. His story demonstrated the independent spirit of fighting through adversity, which I have internalized culturally as a Latino American male. The social work department was a sanctuary for my culturally reverential attitude and ideas. I enrolled in a working with diverse families and individuals course designed to spark our interest in becoming social activists and advocates for civil rights.

My professor in that class chose me and a fellow student to lead a new social work student group called AHANA (Asian, Hispanic, African-American, and Native American). My escape from the cultural anemia of UNCW was putting my energy and enthusiasm into AHANA a culturally diverse organization dedicated to social service projects in the university and greater Wilmington community.

As vice president of AHANA I rolled my sleeves up and organized an event called Project Playground in addition to the Hunger Banquet with the support of OxFam. These successful community events along with hosting culturally relevant movie nights and discussions spurred my identity to be more subgroup identified/Latino identified (Ferdman and Gallegos, 2001). I viewed my Costa Rican heritage as more relevant than my American identity and ardently embraced all aspects of Latino culture.

My East Carolina University (ECU) cultural experience was truly enriching and an exciting three years of my life. ECU has an inviting, loving, and familial atmosphere which made me feel like I belonged. From the moment I stepped on campus to interview for the Master's program until my graduation night I was one cultural thread of the communal quilt that the university weaves each year. I taught others in my program about my background and experiences and instead of feeling out of place amid numerous Caucasian individuals I felt respected and acknowledged for my differences. One example of this was when I began as an admissions counselor at ECU and developed my own Latino student recruiting initiatives.

Mr. Long, My boss at that time was permissive and innovative and encouraged me to develop any projects or recruiting material that could speak to the Latino audience. I began my work in earnest producing a bilingual recruitment brochure geared to attract Latino families and prospective Latino students. In addition, I developed, planned, and executed one of my proudest achievements in my professional career Latino Student Day. I invited about 10-12 families onto the campus and gave them a personal tour of the campus. I arranged for a representative from financial aid, an English professor, and student life reps to communicate their roles in the college as well as field questions from the families about cost, majors, extracurricular activities, and other details that general admission presentations may miss.

During my tenure at ECU I was able to connect with so many optimistic and value building individuals. I actively began seeking out the culturally diverse individuals that I had longed for since my childhood and adolescence. I realized that I needed to be more proactive in seeking diverse and culturally awake individuals instead of waiting them to show up on my doorstep. Some of the people that helped me reflect on myself and become more culturally balanced include a Coharie woman named Paulah, a few Southern belles named Aurora and Claire, an African American colleague nicknamed Pedro, an Athenah/ African-American colleague Bea, and Drs. Wellcome, Pooli, Glad, and Smith at ECU. My ECU experience culminated in my graduation gift from my parents which was a round trip ticket to Costa Rica to learn myself.

December 2007 was an exciting and anxious time for me culturally. I recognized I was transforming into the Introspection stage (Atkinson, Morten, & Sue, 1998) and somewhere between Latino Identified and Latino Integrated (Ferdman & Gallegos, 2001). About a week after graduation I flew down to San Jose, Costa Rica. The anticipation I felt in those four hours could have powered an entire fleet of 747s. My parents had made contact with Tia Clara, an old friend they knew in Heredia, Costa Rica.

Tia Clara and her husband Raul, a native Tico, greeted me outside of *la aduana* (customs) at Juan Santamaria Airport and welcomed me into their Mitsubishi SUV. As we drove through the bustling streets of San Jose I could not help but feel overcome with cultural egocentrism. Seeing the people, tiendas (stores), fincas (farms), and smelling the honeyed air as we passed a variety of panaderias (bakeries) invoked a keen sense of cultural belonging.

That night for dinner I ravished two heaping plates of gallo pinto, the national dish of Costa Rica, along with some fried plantains and a piece of carne asada. As I settled in to the daily rhythm of my two week stay in Costa Rica I began savoring the flavors of daily pura vida. My purpose for my visit was more than to drink in long lost culture but also to go to the hospital where I was born, visit the orphanage where I had been mistreated, and attempt to find my birth parents. My initial hope in doing all of these things was to find answers to burning cultural identity questions and to reconnect with my birth parents as well as siblings, uncles, aunts, and cousins if possible.

My first stop was to go to the actual place of my birth, I was born in Hospital Mexico in the heart of San Jose, Costa Rica. Raul was gracious enough to drive me the next day. As we pulled up I began tearing up as a sense of pride and loss swirled around in my stomach. I examined the hospital as I neared the entrance and thought the place very industrial and somewhat cold with its concrete structural design. An underwhelming building which helped me think of my underwhelming beginning. I entered the hospital and walked around observing doctors and nurses fulfilling their daily rhythms. One part of my heart and soul was content and a piece of my cultural-self puzzle was put together again with this simple act. I strongly believe that in order to be successful in life you must explore your birthplace and origin to know from where you came.

Raul and I decided to then drive to Santa Natalina of Heredia to look for the orphanage where I had spent some of the most difficult years of my life as a child. However, I was saddened and disappointed to learn that the orphanage had been demolished years earlier. I wanted to close the chapter on the soul wounds that I had endured in those tumultuous years. We drove past the original site but it was just a parcel of land with a few bricks and stones strewn brokenly on the ground.

A part of me was content to not see the building but I would have appreciated the opportunity to offer forgiveness to the cold, dank walls and bare rooms that provided shelter to my sister and I prior to our adoption. I said a silent prayer to myself and decided to return to Tia Clara's to journal. Raul and I were planning to go to the Patronato Nacional de la Infancia (Social Services) the following day so I needed to collect my thoughts and feelings to prepare myself.

I woke that morning to pangs of angst and longing and had difficulty eating the gallo pinto and fried eggs for breakfast. My mind kept wandering but I kept repeating to myself, "*this* is why I am here." Raul drove us down to San Jose in his SUV to begin the search for my birth parents. Raul was encouraging me to find out as much as I could on that day in order to make the most of the time I have left. Any moments of internal hesitation were quashed by his guidance and advice. Tia Clara and Raul were practicing Catholics and fully devoted to God's Word and Will. I believe that in those moments and hours Raul was leading me in a spiritual sense. As we checked in to the *Patronato* I took a ticket with a number to be called upon.

An hour later, a warm faced middle age woman with pepper black hair and glasses called my name. Her name was Clara and she was as bright and optimistic as her name signifies. Clara was extremely helpful and listened to my recounting painful childhood experiences of being orphaned and ultimately adopted. I told her that my goal was to not only locate both my parents, if still living, but to also begin putting some of the missing pieces together about my early childhood. She told me all she needed was my birth name and date of birth and she would try to find as much as she could on my family.

Clara found some initial paperwork on both my parents. Ricardo Morales Sanchez and Jovenia Trujillo Hernandez were my parents' names. Most importantly, Clara printed out the social security profile of each one with photos, phone numbers, and addresses (which she was not supposed to do). I held onto those sheets of paper with their photos with fierce determination that I would not lose them. She told us that the rest of the files on my sister and I would have to be collected and organized into a separate file and that would take a couple of days.

As I continued to stare at my birth parents' photos I tuned out most of what Clara was saying and suddenly I felt fearless in seeking my birth parents out. Upon leaving the *Patronato*, Raul and I drove to La Criollita restaurant to dine prior to the next adventure. We agreed that the best plan would be to first call the given number for Ricardo and if available go to Heredia to locate his residence and reunite. The following day we would travel up to Paraisa, Costa Rica which was about four hours away to try to find Jovenia. My hands were shaking as I held Raul's cell phone as it rang for Ricardo. "Aalo" I heard on the other line and I paused before introducing myself. My voice cracked and eyes swelled up as I felt a heavy desperation in my throat. I was overcome with tears and a sense of relief and reclamation as I spoke to my birth father for the first time in about 24 years. I don't recall much of what was said on that day, only the plethora of feelings that jolted me emotionally, psychologically, culturally, and spiritually in those moments.

Raul rescued me from my excited and nonsensical chatter with Ricardo and swiped the phone away to obtain particulars about Ricardo's address and when would be convenient to visit. Ricardo told Raul that he would love to have me stay for dinner and that I was welcome to sleep there as long as I wanted while I was visiting. As Raul and I made our way to Santo Domingo de Heredia, I had a hard time holding back the tears and butterflies dancing all over my body. Raul spun and weaved between the busy streets of Heredia to arrive at the ranch style modest home with a bunch of baby toys strewn all over the front lawn.

I felt my body trembling as Raul and I approached the front

door. On the door hung a family crest with the name Morales. I studied the lavish and ornate details of the green and yellow lettering in old European print. I later learned that the place name Morales is a topographic surname for those living near a hill, stream, church or various trees. The name is originally derived from the Spanish word "Mora" which means mulberry (House of Names). I rang the doorbell in trepidation and awaited the long pause with breath held. Slowly the door opened and in front of me stood a 5'9" slender built man with a white Cuban shirt and black pants. His silvery hair speckled with black in uneven tones. His face was expressive and filled with surprise and joy as he opened his arms and we embraced in a tear filled exchange. I could not do more than cry and snivel and in that moment I felt like a hungry toddler who needed nothing but emotional nourishment.

Ricardo invited me into his home, which he proudly declared 'our' home. He gave me a tour and showed me his room along with my sister, Maria, and brother Alberto's rooms. I also had another sister named Luana who was living with her husband nearby. The only people home at that time was Ricardo and his wife. I still had reservations about her so I was hesitant to engage her in conversation or eye contact. As we spoke Ricardo's wife served us gallo pinto with tortilla and Natilla. After a while Raul stated he had to go and would return the next day to take me to Paraisa. Suddenly, Ricardo's eyes lit up and he told me to tell Jovenia Gracia that he sends his greetings. As the day wore on I learned about Ricardo's work as a plumber for Acueductos & Alcantarillados or A&A as it is known in Costa Rica.

Ricardo took out some picture albums and showed me a couple of pictures of me in Church with Luana and his wife. In the photo I had a haunting look of surprise sitting on the wooden pew. I did note that on the walls of the interior of the home there were numerous photos of Alberto, Luana, and Maria but none of me or Betsy. I asked Ricardo in that moment if he wanted some photos of me to be able to put up, to which he excitedly agreed. I handed him a few photos of me during adolescence, teenage, and early adulthood years from college. He had many questions for me about what I was up to, what was I doing professionally, was I married, and interestingly enough how much money I was making.

That last question turned me off a bit, and I noted his green eyes as if now I was really valuable **only** because of my financial status. I disregarded that feeling because I sensed pride beaming from him as well. We talked about women, soccer, religion, food, and dance. Ricardo was famous in the Santo Domingo precinct for his dancing, and he invited me to dance Salsa with him that night however, I politely declined as I wanted to spend time with my siblings.

Alberto was the first to come home from his university studies and we embraced. He is an avid gamer so he took out some of his game consoles to play some strategy games with me. Alberto was fair skinned with light brown hair almost blonde and had very similar facial features to Ricardo. As we were playing and chatting, both Maria and Luana arrived, Maria from her job at the mall as a security guard and Luana from a day of running errands. We cried, laughed, and mingled until 2 a.m. My heart and mind were overwhelmed with relief, excitement, and curiosity and I fell fast asleep in a bed made just for me. For that brief slice of time I felt I had belonged and was important to my birth father before darkness and peace of night swallowed me over.

The next morning after a tearful goodbye to my siblings and Ricardo, Raul arrived to take me to Paraisa to search for Jovenia Gracia. The drive was approximately three hours to our destination. As we drove west and south around the Pacific Coast of Costa Rica the natural beauty and sumptuous vegetation invited my eyes to feast. The palm trees soared into the sapphire skies with white strokes of puffy clouds.

As we neared Paraisa, Raul and I decided to detour at a nearby beach called Playa Palo Seco. Raul introduced me to his friends who worked at a resort nearby. I took the liberty of taking a stroll on the beach to stretch and listen to the peaceful waves. There was a spiritual connection made between myself and the sand, water, and air on that day. I reflected on how purposeful it would be for me to return to Costa Rica permanently in my later stages of life in order to become one with that land, water, and air.

The sign for Paraisa was nondescript and would have been easy to overlook and drive past. Raul and I suddenly found ourselves off roading on the western coast of Costa Rica. The road to Paraisa was nothing but dirt road, rocks, and palm trees lining both sides of the dirt path. After fifteen minutes we approached a general store with a home attached to it on the back end of the store. Raul spoke in a sincere voice telling me that in the more rural areas there are no street signs or specific numbers assigned to homes. He advised that more likely we would have to ask around in order to find out where Jovenia Gracia resided. He got out of the car and approached the tall, lanky man in the general store. Raul returned to the car excitedly and stated that the tall man was my sister's brother Simon! He knew exactly where to find Jovenia Gracia as well as a few other uncles, aunts, and cousins. Raul and I eagerly drove up the rocky hills of Paraisa towards a big ranch style home with a storage building adjacent to it. I remember only the rush of thoughts and feelings tingling inside of me as we approached my grandfather's home.

As we parked at the bottom of the rocky driveway we slowly climbed towards the ranch style home with wide front porch and as we neared the door, a frail looking older gentleman with permanently bronzed skin, worn blue jeans, and a rancher hat stepped out to assess the commotion. Raul and I introduced ourselves and as I spoke with the gentleman I noticed his eyes open wide and a sudden gush of tears flowed from the inner corners of his eyes. He looked at me with loving, longing eyes and embraced me. He stated that his name was Marco Trujillo and that I could call him, "abuelito" or little grandpa.

Marco led me in to his home and showed me pictures of my grandmother who had passed in 2005. He introduced me to my uncle Celso who was all of 6'4" in height with a slender build and pronounced black mustache. Celso barely spoke and was somewhat distant and cautious about engaging socially. He wore green farmer boots with soiled pants and a red, thin, checkered shirt. Next to Celso was my Uncle Eduardo and I learned that Celso worked in the fincas (farms) around Paraisa along with Uncle Eduardo. Eduardo was much shorter in stature, with a black mustache, and wistful eyes. He was dressed in a farmer's shirt, tattered blue jeans, and tall black rain boots that were almost as tall as he was. We shook hands and greeted each other and Eduardo asked me questions about my journey and how I was enjoying my visit to Costa Rica. It felt as if he were speaking for the both of them.

Marco asked me to sit down on the porch with him on one of his traditional, wooden rocking chairs overlooking the rural beauty of Paraisa which was relatively untouched by modern engineering and industry. Marco began our conversation by recounting how tragic the circumstances around my abandonement were. He explained that he never would have let me suffer in an orphanage if he had known what Ricardo had been up to in 1984 and early 1985. I asked him to further clarify because I had just spent some time with him prior to my trip to Paraisa. According to Marco, he and Jovenia Gracia learned of Betsy and I's abandonment a month after Ricardo had dropped the both of us off at the Patronato Civil and signed the final paperwork. In that moment the feeling of betrayal cut deep and a flood of rage engulfed me. I stood up and stormed down the rocky hill, needing to make sense of what I had just heard. (Later upon returning to San Jose and speaking directly with employees of the Patronato Civil this account was confirmed).

As I walked along a gravel path tasting the saltiness of bitter tears swimming on my lips I recalled a Victor Frankl quote about challenging the meaning of life being the truest form of being a human. I continued walking and witnessed the beauty of the palm and ceiba trees on both sides of the rocky path defining a pathway and speaking to me as if to say, "the road you are on is *your* road despite the uncertainty of what is around the corner." I sat on the edge of the cliff of a gravelly hill and stared into the amazing azure sky and placid river beneath it. The river and sky in that moment appeared to be in perfect unity following each other's missions in the natural world. I don't remember how long I sat there in quiet meditation but it probably was a few hours as the sky began to bronze when I finally turned around and went back to sit down with Grandpa Marco and told him that I wanted to know more about him and Jovenia Gracia.

He told me where Jovenia Gracia was living and that maybe it would be best for me to visit her and spend some time with her. I agreed with his venerable wisdom and he told me that when Marco returned from work it would be a great idea for the both of us to visit Jovenia Gracia and surprise her. I asked him who Martin was and he said that he was my brother and I also had a brother named Sebastien who was living in Heredia with his stepmother, and my youngest brother's name was Donal who lived with a wealthy family in Quepos. I learned that Martin's father died before he was born so Marco took him in and has been raising him all this time. Sebastien's father was a violent drunk and he abused Jovenia Gracia until she decided to get away from him.

Sebastien stayed with his father through his father remarrying a lady named Lara but soon that marriage ended and Sebastien decided to stay with Lara who took him in as her own. I instantly wanted to return to Heredia in that moment to visit Sebastien; I promised myself to see him prior to returning to the States. Martin and Sebastien visited each other often and enjoyed each other's company. They would usually meet up during holidays and vacation weeks. Donal had been adopted by a wealthy family in Quepos the day he was born. Martin and Donal had known each other for a while but were not close from what I could tell. As I understand it, the wife of a prominent businessman was unable to give birth and so they entered an agreement with Jovenia Gracia that they would be able to have her next child. More than likely this agreement was not resolved by the proper governmental channels but it did not matter because Jovenia Gracia was classified an unfit mother in the eyes of her family and the social circles in Paraisa. As such Donal was handed over on the day of his birth to a new mother and father with means as his new father was a successful business owner in hardware and tools.

Martin walked in to Marco's home and from his eyes I could tell he had been holding back tears for a while and we embraced so tightly and genuinely it was as if we had always been connected metaphysically. We did not have to say anything to each other, the look in each other's eyes spoke volumes for all the frustration, uncertainty, joy, belonging, and sadness that we experienced. I kept staring at Martin seeing pieces of myself in his eyes, nose, ears, forehead, and smile. We agreed to make the 30 minute walking journey across town to visit with Jovenia Gracia. We crossed the Rio Las Vegas along the way as we talked about life, soccer, women, Jovenia Gracia, and deeply philosophical things like would we be connected in the spirit world since God did not provide the opportunity for us in our births...

As we approached Jovenia Gracia's house I felt a calming sense of forgiveness touch my heart. As I write this now I imagine her hesitancy and feelings of guilt and shame that must have been building up knowing I was in town. Her front door was painted bright crimson and the walls were coated in a beautiful teal color. Jovenia Gracia answered the door and I longingly stared at her face and focused on the gravity of the moment.

This was my final emotional tempest of the day but it was the most overpowering and I was at a loss of words for 15 minutes as my throat felt constricted and I was just focused on breathing and remaining conscious. Jovenia spoke with a mild slur and Martin had to interpret for me at times because I could not fully understand her. Her tears felt real to me whereas I did begin to question Ricardo's tears.

It was getting late and I was exhausted from all of the day's events. Marco and I agreed to stay there that night so I could be around our birth mother and get to know her. Jovenia Gracia and I sat together on her modest couch and enjoyed each other's company with minimal communication. I observed that she had dentures and remember thinking that she seemed young to have dentures. She began telling me some interesting facts about me.

She told me that I was an easy birth and that I was born in the afternoon at 2:52 in Hospital Mexico in Caja Uruca San Jose. She said that the first two years with Ricardo were great and that I had received a lot of love and attention until he met his current wife and decided he wanted no more to do with her. As soon as Betsy was born the relationship began going south and she was left to pick up the pieces when he left her to marry another woman.

I discovered that I was named for a handsome telenovela actor named Danny. Jovenia Gracia explained that she was heartbroken when she understood what Ricardo had done and asked me forgiveness. In that moment a slight cool breeze pinched our noses and we embraced. I did not have any tears left that night but strangely they would have been tears of reclamation and not necessarily of hurt and pain.

The following morning Jovenia Gracia cooked us some delicious gallo pinto with fried eggs and handmade tortillas. I watched in delight as Jovenia Gracia mashed the Masa Harina mixture into round flat corn tortillas. She pounded and rolled the Masa with the earnest skill of many years. She placed the beautiful, white, and round tortillas on the skillet in her kitchen and flipped them over after a minute or two and they were ready to devour. As I admired her culinary skills I began talking to her about loss. Specifically, about how she has not raised any of her five children and I spoke to her about how traumatic that is and how much it would help her to talk and process the pain and loss with a psychologist and she agreed that she would give it a try. I have since been helping her pay for monthly sessions with a psychologist in Quepos in order for her to begin a new more meaningful chapter personally, psychologically, and emotionally. During our conversation I learned that she had also been a black sheep in the family and was not always treated with as much love and respect as she had deserved from Marco and Ana. This helped me understand part of the reason why Gracia had always wanted to be independent and not ask for help even in times when she truly needed help from her family. I believe there are dark family secrets between Gracia and Marco but she is not willing to disclose at this time. Every time I would ask her about her relationship with Marco she hesitated and tried to change the subject quickly.

After breakfast, Marco and I decided that our plan for the rest of the day would be to venture by bus to Quepos and pick Donal up and by the time we got back Marco would be arriving from a bus in Heredia so all four of us could be together for the next few days. It was an exciting day ahead and as Marco and I neared Quepos he told me that all of the aunts, uncles and cousins would meet tonight at Tia Daniela's home to watch a soccer game and eat dinner. The prospect of meeting so many new family members was exciting and overwhelming and the anticipation had my stomach in knots.

Arriving in Quepos we got off the bus stop and walked a few blocks to an opulent neighborhood where all homes were sizable and furnished with at least one or two car garages. We rang the doorbell to my brother Donal's home and his mother answered politely and ushered us in. Donal came out of his room and hugged Martin and I and we commenced with Karaoke to break the ice.

Donal was portly, tall, with dark beady eyes and a prominent black mustache. He welcomed us to sit down on his white leather sofas and turned on his large screen TV to commence playing his favorite Super Karaoke Hits DVD. Donal insisted that we all take turns singing classics like Feliz Navidad!, Baby Got Back, Like a Prayer, and San Francisco. Interestingly enough, Donal knew all the lyrics to all the songs by heart but did not really understand what they meant necessarily which I thought was hilarious at the time.

One thing I observed about Donal was that he did not get visually emotional to see me and seemed to prefer to maintain his distance either to lack of trust or potentially autistic mannerisms. Donal did not want to talk about Jovenia Gracia and preferred to talk about the material things he had accumulated over time. I learned that Donal was an excellent artist and he was proud to show Martin and I some of his work. He presented me with a beautiful painting of a small boat anchored on a beautiful tropical beach with the sun sparkling over the ocean. I keep the painting in my home as a reminder of that wonderful and exhilarating time with my brothers.

We enjoyed a hearty lunch of steak and olla de carne prior to leaving for Paraisa. Donal was gracious enough to drive us in his red Mitsubishi Montero back to Paraisa. On the way he pumped some Reggae ton and we jammed all the way back to Paraisa just savoring each other's company. I could not help but appreciate all the small details of Donal's mustache, the 8 ball shifter, and the funkadelic seat covers in his Montero.

Back at the Trujillo Reunion everyone was there including Tia Daniela and her children Ranjel and Belinda, Tia Paola and her children Tony, Carly, Mike, and Ron, Tia Marina and her children Penelope, Walter, and Karrie, Tio Brayan and his children Alan and Mary, Tio Elon and his daughter Dannie, Tio Saul and his children Jorge and Arlia, and Tio Celso who has no children. The only uncle I did not meet was Tio Horatio and his children Maria and Kevino. I reflected on the irony of having felt alone many times during my life journey in the United States and now I was presented with an entire town of Trujillo family.

The air wafted with the tantalizing scents of a Costa Rican celebration including gallo pinto, arroz con pollo, tamales, handmade corn tortillas, caramel, horchata, frescos, flan and tres leches cake. All of the food was homemade and absolutely delicious. After eating, my brothers and I, along with Rangel and Ron decided to play some three on three soccer under the dying orange sun over the Paraisa landscape. This memory will forever stick in my mind as precious and sacred.

I felt self-actualized in those moments of uniting with my brothers and playing barefoot soccer with makeshift goals and a timeworn soccer ball. It was a defining moment in my life and helped me reflect on the importance of learning about myself and exploring the deeper aspects of my culture. That night before I fell asleep I looked outside the bedroom window of Marco's house and studied the brilliance of the stars plastered against a blood deep onyx and discovered the satisfaction of knowing with unshakeable certainty who I really was...I had attained my own experience of transcending the introspection stage and arriving very close to synergetic articulation and awareness in those few days in the mountains of Paraisa.

One of my heroes in counseling is Carl Rogers and it was during this cultural self-adventure that his words became palpable and tangible for my life:

> *The good life is a process not a state of being. It is a direction, not a destination (Rogers, 1961, p.186).*

> *For the vast majority of persons who do not have an optimal childhood there is hope for change and development toward psychological maturity... whereby the individual continues to dissolve the conditions of worth, achieve a self congruent with experience and restore the organismic valuing process (Rogers, 1959).*

> *Based on the above excerpts from Rogers, the following affirmations are based on the experience of my life and writing this book...*

> *The self is congruent and whole with experience based on the ongoing struggle of obtaining emotional, psychological, cultural, spiritual, academic, economic and adaptive resilience alongside a harmonious purpose and meaning in life.*

Resiliencies are like booster packs and knowing when to pick the right one/combination when you need it in any given moment is crucial to meaning making.

Finally, repeat these affirmations to yourself each day borrowed from Deepak Chopra (1994):
I believe in myself
I love myself
I was born for special reasons
I have unique gifts and talents that no one else has and my job is to discover what those are
Today I will find ways to help others

Meaning journal. Please begin incorporating cultural elements into your meaning journal. The hope is that this chapter has helped you reflect on your own cultural trials and triumphs. Use the following prompt to get you started: I will bring purpose, meaning, worth, and cultural reflection to myself and others through my thoughts, feelings, and actions today by....You may choose to write down a sentence or a whole page in the journal during this time. The beauty of journaling is that it allows you to organize your thoughts and feelings into a tangible portrait of themes and subthemes of your life. When you recognize themes in your life that are preventing you from being more resilient in some feature of your life then you can begin changing your attitude, thoughts, feelings, and behaviors about that area of your life to promote positive change. As you continue to add to your meaning journal don't be surprised if you end up with a book as that would be a tributary reason you are reading this book...

References

Atkinson, D. R., Morten, G, & Sue, D. W. (Editors) (1998). *Counseling American minorities: A cross-cultural perspective* (5th ed.). McGraw-Hill Company

Brown, G. C. (2013). *Latino voices: A qualitative study of first generation college Latino males.* (Doctoral Dissertation). Retrieved from http://search.proquest.com/docview/1494147425 (3608268)

Chopra, D. (1994). The seven spiritual laws of success. San Rafael: CA Amber-Allen Publishing

Clauss-Ehlers, C. (2004). *Cultural resilience.* Encyclopedia of Cross Cultural School Psychology. Retrieved September 14, 2015 from http://link.springer.com/referenceworkentry/10.1007%2F978-0-387-71799-9_115#

Henderson, N (2015). The resiliency quiz. Retrieved July 13, 2015 from http://www.edu.gov.mb.ca/k12/cur/cardev/gr12_found/blms/1-3.pdf

Ball, Philip (2014). *Make your own memories: One day you will be able to replace the good ones with the bad ones.* Retrieved June 1, 2015 from http://www.theguardian.com/science/2014/oct/12/memory-how-science-fiction-can-become-reality

Cowan, N. (2008). *What are the differences between long-term, short-term, and working memory?* Prog Brain Res. 169 323-338. Doi: 10.1016/S0079-6123(07)00020-9

Ferdman, B. M., & Gallegos, P. I. (2001). Racial identity development and Latinos in the United States. In C. L. Wijeyesinghe & B. W. Jackson, III (Eds.), *New perspectives on Racial Identity Development: A theoretical and practical anthology* (pp. 32-66). New York: New York University Press.

Geraerts, E., & McNally, R. J. (2008). Forgetting unwanted memories: Direct forgetting and thought suppression methods. Acta Psychologica, 127, 614-622. doi: 10.1016/j.actpsy.2007.11.003

House of Names (2015). Retrieved November 24, 2015 from https://www.houseofnames.com/Morales-family-crest

Jung, C. G. (1964). Man and his symbols. New York: Doubleday.

Kim J. (1981) The process of Asian American identity development from Sue, et al. (1998). Multicultural Counseling Competencies: Individual and Organizational Development. Sage Productions. Thousand Oaks, CA.

Morales, E. E. (2008). *Exceptional female students of color: Academic resilience and gender in higher education.* Innovative Higher Education, *33*, 197-213. doi: 10.1007/s10755-008-9075-y

Oberg, K. (1960). Cultural shock: Adjustment to new cultural environments. *Practical Anthropology, 7,* 77-82.

Rampell, C. (2013). It takes a B.A to find a job as a file clerk. Retrieved April 25, 2017 from www.nytimes.com/2013/02/20/business/college-degree-required-by-increasing-number-of-companies.html

Rogers, C. (1959). A theory of therapy, personality and interpersonal relationships as developed in the client-centered framework. In (ed.) S. Koch, *Psychology: A study of a science. Vol. 3: Formulations of the person and the social context.* New York: *McGraw Hill.*

Rogers, C. R. (1961). *On becoming a person: A psychotherapists view of psychotherapy.* Boston: *Houghton Mifflin.*

Stevenson, B. (2014). *Just mercy: a story of justice and redemption.* New York: *Spiegel & Grau.*

Zolli, A. & Healy, A. M. (2012). *Resilience: Why things bounce back.* New York: *Free Press.*